I0130090

America In Focus:
The Stunning View Through A Two-Way Mirror

Robert J Burgess
aka The Focus Group Guy[TM]

MA Arts

MA Arts Publishing, LLC
Littleton, Colorado 80128

www.americainfocusthebook.com

www.marketingadvocates.com

Copyright © 2008 by MA Arts Publishing, LLC
http://www.maartspublishing.com

All rights reserved. No part of this book may be reproduced or
transmitted in any form or by any means, electronic or mechanical,
including photocopying, recording, or by any information storage and
retrieval system, without permission in writing from the Publisher.

ISBN 978-0-578-00162-3
© 2008 MA Arts Publishing, LLC
All rights reserved.
Library of Congress Control Number: 2008911183

It's Focus Group Night In America!

(Continued From Back Cover…)

…Each year, billions of dollars are spent conducting **focus groups** across the United States. Major corporations, political leaders, advertising agencies, small businesses, labor unions, government agencies – and even churches – pay for the privilege of sitting in darkened rooms across the country and eavesdropping on their invited guests from behind a two-way mirror. From this vantage point, they listen and glean insights into what Americans **really** think on everything from the legislative agenda in Washington to the shapes of marshmallows in a box of Lucky Charms.

Indeed, what people have to say behind closed doors in focus groups has a profound impact on our daily lives:

- Whether corporations should sink billions of dollars into developing new technologies such as wireless phone services, Video-On-Demand, or iPods.

- Which ads a major political candidate should use to entice voters during their run for office.

- Which ending of a major Hollywood movie will make it to the screen of the local multi-plex, and which will end up on the cutting room floor.

- Whether new fashion styles will make their way from the runways of Paris to the center aisle of Walmart.

- Whether a major new beer will be dark and full-flavored, or light and drinkable.

And that's merely the tip of the iceberg.

It's often said that information is power – so imagine how powerful **you'd** be if you could harness the data from tens of thousands of focus group participants at one time. Think about what you'd learn if **you** could sit behind the mirror and listen to everything from how Americans spend money to how they plan to vote in the next election. It's **all** fair game in focus groups – favorite TV shows, their dreams, doubts, finances, race relations, religion, morality, romance – even your favorite Lucky Charms marshmallow shape!

Now, Robert J. Burgess, the country's leading focus group moderator, has lifted the veil of secrecy and invites **you** to take a front row seat behind the two-way mirror. *"America In Focus: The Stunning View Through A Two-Way Mirror"* is based on a decades-long odyssey of more than 2,000 focus groups. *"America In Focus"* will help readers to understand:

- That a New American Dream is shaping our economy as Baby Boomers head toward their "golden years" and Gen X settles into Middle Age.

- How Big Media is dying – and with it, the traditional advertising industry.

- How "Management By Chaos" – or MBC – dominates the American workplace and pervades our business culture, leading to surging levels of stress, ineffective management and strong job dissatisfaction.

- How the "politics of cynicism" influences our view of government and our political leaders, and has cast a long shadow at the ballot box.

- The rise of the "Springer Generation" has led to a general decline in morality, civility and culture.

- That "villainy" is supplanting traditional hero worship in establishing social trends.

What you read in *America In Focus* may cause you to laugh, cry, scratch your head in wonder or amazement, or maybe even jump for joy. Regardless, when the journey is done, you'll know a different kind of America…an *"America In Focus."*

Acknowledgements

☆ ☆ ☆ ☆ ☆

There are four individuals to whom I will be eternally indebted – without them, America would never quite come into focus.

First, I would like to thank my editor at MA Arts, Pamela Burgess. In many ways, Pam is the dream editor all writers fantasize about. On the one hand, she is very engaged and hard working. But on the other, she gives authors space, and even thinks like an author. She has improved this manuscript immeasurably. Thanks, Pam.

I also must thank my parents, John and Doris, for all of their love and support. One could argue that whatever talent I have, I owe to my parents. But beyond that, they have been incredibly inspirational on *America In Focus*, constantly providing encouragement when things seemed darkest. They've also been more involved in reading and reviewing the manuscript than anyone except my Editor. In short, they've been there for me, every step of the way. I can never repay Mom and Dad for all they've done for me, my whole life. All I can really say is, "Thanks" and "I love you both." Again, without Mom and Dad, there would simply be no book.

Finally, I must thank my colleague at Marketing Advocates, Inc., the consulting firm where I work, Deb Teter. Deb has done everything needed to keep this project on track, from cracking jokes, to research and manuscript review. I can't imagine how many hours she's worked on this project. But it's not an exaggeration to say that without Deb, there would be no book. And special thanks to Deb's husband, Bill, and her family, for allowing her to work so much on this book instead of her roles as mom and wife. I am forever grateful that Deb can try to balance so much, and that the Teters are so patient.

Special thanks to the staff at Able Printing & Graphics, especially Sue Floyd and Steve Tolle, for designing the cover to the book – a true work of art!

And thanks to the thousands of focus group participants from my focus groups. I can't recall most of them individually, but I have tremendous respect for the people we've spoken to, over the years. Again, without them, there would be no book.

And thanks to you, dear readers. I really do hope that this book will be so enjoyable and informative as to influence your lives, in some small way. Enjoy!

★ ★ ★ ★ ★

Robert J Burgess

Littleton, CO

(August, 2008)

The Verdict On Robert J. Burgess'

"Silver Bullets":

"One of the year's ten best business books."
—Fort Worth Star-Telegram

"A persuasive black-humor business saga."
—Publisher's Weekly

"'Silver Bullets' is an entertaining look at why things can go very wrong."
—Jack Trout, Best-Selling Author

"Many inside-story books claim to be 'wickedly funny.' This one actually is."
—Dale Dauten, Nationally Syndicated
Business Columnist

"Writing with humor and incredulity…Burgess' writing is entertaining."
—Shirley Presber, The Virginian Pilot & The Ledger-Star

"Recommended for both lay readers and specialists."
—Library Journal

Table Of Contents

Author's Notes

⋆ ⋆ ⋆ ⋆ ⋆

Throughout this text, verbatim quotes from actual focus group respondents have been used to illustrate the tone and substance of focus group discussions. In order to protect the identities of respondents and preserve the integrity of the focus group research, the identities of these respondents are not disclosed in this book – they are safely tucked away in our company's secure vaults.

At times, the accounts from focus groups and the subsequent analysis are referred to in the plural ("we"), rather than the singular ("I"). This reflects the fact that even though the author is usually the moderator of our company's focus groups, we do sometimes use other moderators, and use personnel other than myself to watch and analyze focus groups. In other words, this reflects the fact that the author is employed by Marketing Advocates, Inc., a full-service marketing consulting firm located in Denver, CO.

To my adorable niece, Emily, and my

hockey superstar nephew, Thomas:

I hope we are good stewards of this planet

until your generation arrives.

Introduction:

Through The Looking

Glass Darkly

✮ ✮ ✮ ✮ ✮

Have you ever wondered, really wondered, what you might accomplish in life, if **only** you could see into people's minds and do a better job of predicting the future? Perhaps you'd place a bet at the race track, do a better job of choosing stocks, get promoted at work, pick the right person to marry, buy a new house in a soon-to-be-fashionable neighborhood, invest in a new business, join the campaign of a rising politician…okay, okay, so predicting the future seems like nothing more than a flight of fancy, a dreamy delusion.

But imagine for a moment if you **could** do a better job of seeing into the future, but not with perfect accuracy, and not with the help of tea leaves, or a soothsayer, or by reading the lines on the palm of your hand. Imagine, instead, that you understood what millions of Americans were **really** thinking…not just family, co-workers, or the people who live on your block, but the **whole country**. Understanding what's on people's minds on this grand scale would be invaluable as you navigated the troubled waters of life; accurate insight as to what the future might be could influence many critical aspects of your day-to-day life, including career, family, business, economics, and even politics.

Two centuries ago, Alexis de Tocqueville had just such an opportunity as he traveled on horseback from cityscape to countryside, talking to Americans of all shapes, sizes, ages, rank and privilege. By talking to its citizens, he had set out to understand the forces that had given birth to America's grand experiment with democracy, and to understand what the future held for this noble concept. His epic book, **Democracy In America,** proved so insightful that it's still standard reading in political science and history classes, and his predictions of a bright future for the country and its citizens have proven to be prescient. As de Tocqueville knew only too well two centuries ago, getting to really know Americans was to know our future as a people, a country, and a society.

So imagine the power and influence if you, like de Tocqueville, could travel across the country, meeting and talking with thousands of Americans, face-to-face. Imagine that these meetings and conversations were more – much more – than a cursory greeting and handshake. What would you know about the future if you could sit across the table from the thousands of people, look them in the eye, and ask about everything from how they planned to vote to how they spend money? What insights about the future could be gleaned by asking tens of thousands of American about their dreams, worries, finances, race relations, religion, morality, romance, child rearing, education, and even their sexual fantasies? Imagine for a moment that all of these topics and many more were fair game. Think about all you'd learn and how valuable that information would be in understanding the future - the worlds of commerce, public policy, government, family, and education, in our day-to-day lives.

Like de Tocqueville, I've truly been blessed in that I need not imagine such conversations with Americans – I've actually lived them. For nearly two decades, the author has traveled the country from coast to coast, big cities to small towns, talking to Americans from all walks of life. In my capacity as a professional market researcher, a wide variety of companies, from start-ups to blue-chip behemoths, as well as educational institutions, government agencies and public policy groups, have hired my firm to find out what makes Americans tick. In this role, we've spent literally "tens of thousands" of hours in deep conversations during focus groups and in-depth interviews, while our clients peered in and watched through smoky, two-way mirrors as Americans revealed everything from what they'd eaten for lunch that day to their deepest, darkest secrets.

America In Focus: The Stunning View Through A Two-Way Mirror reflects this two decade journey of discovery, a vivid mosaic of this country, its citizens and the future. In this era marked by deep skepticism, rising cynicism, charges of a "biased" media, and the growing influence of Internet journalism, *America In Focus* is a portrait of the future painted with the least filtered and most basic source of information: the thoughts, opinions and experiences of everyday Americans obtained in face-to-face interviews.

The current era is often dubbed the "Information Age," as we are literally awash in bits of information about every conceivable topic. But two factors lend *America In Focus* its wholly unique perspective. First, it's based on a very simple premise: To learn what people are thinking, one must first ask questions, and then **listen**. Or, to paraphrase one of our clients from the early years, "You'll be surprised what people will tell you, if only you ask." As market researchers, we've been granted the unique privilege or license to ask literally a million different questions of strangers over the years, from the trite to the very pointed and controversial. Accordingly, we are greatly indebted to citizens across the country who have exhibited seemingly limitless patience, thoughtfulness and honesty in answering our questions.

The second factor which lends *America In Focus* its unique perspective is that it's based upon the **collective wisdom** of tens of thousands of Americans interviewed over the past two decades. As Emerson wrote in his *Letters & Social Aims*, "Our knowledge is the amassed thought and experience of innumerable minds." In other words, while we'd love to wear the mantle of "genius" or "experts" in writing this book and describing a vision for the future, we're merely messengers. *America In Focus* is, at its core, a self-portrait of the country and its citizens. Best of all, our sources for this vision of the future aren't Hollywood stars, "talking head experts" from cable TV, or the so-called media elite, but a genuine cross-section of America, or what self-proclaimed populist Bill O'Reilly often calls "the folks."

In a country as diverse and complex as the United States, a book such as *America In Focus* must reflect this rich tapestry and address a wide variety of topics. Whether your interests lie in commerce, politics, education, health care, entertainment, religion, family life – or any other interests in a list too long to enumerate here – we believe that thinking about, anticipating, and, indeed, even understanding what Americans are really thinking will,, in some way, make your life better.

Thinking about the value of seeing the future more clearly today, high-tech expert Alfred Mercer once wrote, "There was a man in the East whose constant prayer was that he might see today with the eyes of tomorrow." It is hoped that after reading *America In Focus*, you will feel, at least with regard to seeing the future, as if the prayer to which Mercer referred has been answered.

Chapter 1:

The New American Dream

★ ★ ★ ★ ★

"You watch, man. Some day I am going to hit the lottery. And when I do, I am going to have so much bling that everyone will just have to kiss my a--."
–Brian L., 16, High School Sophomore, Parsippany, New Jersey

"Shoot. Money is everything these days. It determines the quality of your life in this country, for sure."
–Edna, 39, Retailer, Pittsburgh, PA

The American Dream

Quiz shows are the ultimate American invention, so it somehow seems appropriate to begin our journey through America with a quiz. Ready? Here goes.

Question: What do the following names have in common?

- Dennis Kozlowski
- Martha Stewart
- Suzanne Mullins
- Howard K. Stern
- Terrell Owens
- Barry Bonds
- Jeffrey Skilling
- Joe Francis
- The 1995 Steinmetz High School (Chicago, IL) Academic Decathlon Team

Give up? So easily?

Answer: They are all symbols – "poster children" really – for "The New American Dream," a radical change in our country's values and ideals that is having a profound impact on the way we live. (We'll provide more detail on this infamous list above later in the chapter.)

The "American Dream" is a somewhat subjective term; it likely originated with author James Trulow Adams in his book, *The Epics Of America*, early in the 20th Century.[1] And yet, most of us have a general idea as to what it means.

In simple terms, the American Dream refers to the United States as a land of vast opportunity in which people of all races, creeds and all walks of life are free to pursue prosperity through hard work, entrepreneurship and traditional economic values, such as thriftiness. In stark contrast to Europe's gentrified system in which most wealth is possessed by a relative few – the aristocrats – and passed on from generation to generation, our American Dream has traditionally allowed anyone, at any time, to pursue freedom and prosperity. Today, you could be struggling and down to your last dime, and tomorrow, well, who knows? It's never been a stretch for Americans to leap from "rags to riches." To many, that's the ultimate Dream. And in stark contrast to most of the rest of the world, Americans have been free and prosperous for our first 200+ years as a country.

The Dream has shaped and influenced many aspects of American life for more than two centuries. For instance, our country has traditionally been one of the most productive on earth, in part because of the strong work ethic that's part of The Dream: work hard, and you will eventually prosper. We've also traditionally been very entrepreneurial, taking economic risks and pursuing prosperity with abandon, in search of

---

[1] From Wikipedia's online encyclopedia.

The Dream. (Think of J.P. Morgan, Henry Ford, and Bill Gates, to name but a few of our great American entrepreneurs over the past two centuries.)

Home ownership has been another integral part of this Dream. We Americans saved and bought homes, paying for this most prized asset with long mortgages, often thirty years or more, because we believed in ourselves and our ability to live the Dream. (Many Americans have traditionally spoken of the Dream as being nothing more than a white picket fence surrounding their very own home.)

Thriftiness has also figured prominently in this Dream, driven by our quest for prosperity and financial security. Traditionally, even average, middle-class Americans saved money into "nest eggs" throughout their working lives, enabling them to retire to a life of prosperous leisure, able to pass on wealth to the next generation. We've been able to invest money into the stock market, becoming paper millionaires in mere days during bull markets like the technology boom of the late 1990's, and sometimes crying in our beer over losses that wiped us out (recall The Great Depression). Borrowing, saving and investing, with virtually no restriction on **who** could participate; to most of the rest of the world, this, too, has been a Dream.

And the Dream hasn't just been economic in nature. Despite recent strife in this country (covered in later chapters), many have spoken in glowing terms about the U.S. offering racial and social equality to all, an egalitarian society without rank and privilege. Still others have spoken about the American Dream as representing our vast and virtually unlimited freedoms – of speech, the press, even the freedom to traverse the fifty states without limitation – which we cherish and sometimes fight to preserve.

Whatever your personal notion of the American Dream, focus groups indicate that virtually **everyone** has some knowledge of, and interest in, the Dream; it's a nearly **universal concept**.

> *"I think we all dream about owning a home, don't we?"*
> —John L., 41, Sales Representative, Edison, NJ

> *"We [Americans] always talk about an 'American Dream,' with the white picket fence, and the house, and the family and such."*
> —Sandy, 31, Student/Housewife, El Cajon, CA

> *"The American Dream? Shoot, I'm living it."*
> —Derek, 24, Grocery Clerk, Grand Junction, CO

However, focus groups indicate that the American Dream has changed **radically** over the past ten years. And with this re-casting of The Dream, we've also seen abrupt changes in our values, ideals, our outlook on the future, the economy, and even changes in social patterns (how we relate to each other).

Later in this chapter, we'll outline some potential reasons for the shift in our collective Dream, and how it's impacting our country. But first, we need to come to some common understanding of this New Dream, which we find in focus groups to be remarkably consistent across all areas of the country, and across all socio-economic groups. Quite simply, the **New American Dream is**:

Get Rich Or Die Trying…Now!!!

This New Dream represents not just change, but radical change, and can be more readily understood in the words of actual Americans:

"Shoot. Michael Milken went to prison for a year or two, and he still walked away with a billion dollars. I'd make that deal again in a second. A billion dollars for one or two years of my life? You bet I'd do that."
—John, 44, Bus Driver, Miami, FL

"I will do whatever it takes – and I mean that – whatever – to provide for my family. I don't care if it's legal or not."
—Sally, 32, Administrative Assistant, Los Angeles, CA

"All that matters when you die is how much money you had."
—Smitty, 28, Student, South San Francisco, CA

"I want to get rich right away so that I can retire and kick back. It's pretty easy to do. But I want to get rich right now, not when I'm old."
—Jen, 22, Receptionist, Salt Lake City, UT

It's necessary to dig beneath the surface in order to more fully understand this New Dream, so that we can better assess how it's impacting our country. For starters, there are several components of this **New** American Dream, or what some might eventually come to think of as a nightmare.

Components of the New American Dream

Americans <u>crave</u> financial success/wealth.

In the quest for money and wealth, anything goes. <u>Anything</u>.

Americans want to build wealth <u>right</u> <u>now</u>!

1. Americans _crave_ financial success/wealth.

While becoming prosperous was most assuredly part of the Old American Dream, the New Dream involves going well beyond prosperity to acquiring **vast sums of wealth**, or becoming **rich**. Americans now have become obsessively money-hungry and materialistic; shopping is the penultimate American leisure time pursuit. We now work to earn, and live to spend what we earn. (It's worth noting that a standard focus group warm-up question involves asking respondents to name their favorite leisure time pursuits. After more than 2,000 focus groups, I've yet to do a group where shopping **wasn't** mentioned.)

> *"I want to be flat-out rich, so that I have security."*
> —Jill, 56, Real Estate, Louisville, KY

> *"Money isn't everything...but I guess it really is everything. It's damned important. Everything else flows from how much money you have, when you get down to it.."*
> —John, 38, Educator, Seattle, WA

> *"Do we really need all the stuff we have? Yeah, I think so, if we're going to live comfortably."*
> —Eljibe, 28, Internet Specialist, New Have, CT

> *"I want to grow up and be rich!"*
> —Sally, 9, 3rd Grade, Jackson, MS

It's almost surprising that nine year-old Sally (in the quote above) didn't use the term "comfortable" in her childlike declaration, now that it's become our national, guilt-free euphemism for being "rich." Our focus groups indicate that Americans are at ease with acknowledging their interest in not just being prosperous, but being flat-out rich. (But we still cling to calling it "comfortable," rather than rich.)

And Americans have no trouble rationalizing this goal, citing everything from the need for "security" to the need to pay for (our children's) college educations in recognizing this quest for money.

On our journey across America, we've documented America's obsession with becoming "comfortable," or rich, and attempted to summarize some of the major changes in our views on money in the following chart.

Money & The New American Dream

What's In	What's Out
• Retirement planning	• Saving money
• Flipping houses	• (Low yield) Savings bonds
• Stock trading	• Honesty
• Trading up to a bigger house	• Modesty
• Financing a big car over 7 years	• Saving over time for big purchases
• Rating mutual fund firms	• Earning your way to the top
• Conspicuous consumption	• Savings accounts
• Immediate gratification	• Retiring comfortably
• Starting out at the top	• Patience
• Retiring early/young	• Living within your means
• Retiring rich	
• Infomercials on wealth building	

Oink. Oink. The New American Dream doesn't involve prosperity, but building **vast** wealth, as even the wealthy want to get still richer. Turn back to the list that opened this chapter, the poster children for the New American Dream. Dennis Kozlowski and Jeffrey Skilling defrauded investors in their respective companies (Tyco and Enron) in order to line their own pockets. Of course, they were already rich at the time, but they simply wanted **more** money. Martha Stewart traded in her spatulas and herbs for knowledge used to cook up illegal insider stock trades. She was worth anywhere from a quarter billion to a full billion dollars at the time, but no matter. She was rich, but she wanted **more!** And who can forget Howard K. Stern – not the shock jock, but the barracuda barrister who was practically glued to Anna Nicole Smith in her final years. Stern wasn't content with the money he and Smith had accumulated (they were shopping for a yacht on the day she died). No, Stern lied on a baby's birth certificate about his paternity, peddled pictures of his dead companion's bedroom within hours of her death, and sold tear-jerking interviews to tabloid TV about the "love" of his life, all in a pathetic attempt to horn in on the estimated half-billion dollar fortune that Dannielynn Smith, Anna's baby, will inherit some day. He just wanted **more!**

Our obsession with money runs deep. Recently, we ran across a young, high school senior from Arizona in our focus groups, to whom learning and acquiring knowledge are anathema. This young man and his dad care little about such pedantic matters as learning and education. No, they view college purely as vocational (work force) training, and their viewpoints are far from exceptional or outside the norms. They **are** the norms:

"I want to go to college to get rich. I want to major in something that will pay off in a big way. I've already learned what I need to. Now, it's all about the big bucks. And partying, too."
—Paul, 18, Graduating Senior, Scottsdale, AZ

"I want him to go to college so he can get a great job. I really don't care what he learns, as long as he can make a lot of money. An awful lot."
—Paul's Father, 53, Business Executive, Scottsdale, AZ

And if you're confused and think that college has always been about landing that great job, think again. Once upon a time, we actually valued learning as its own pursuit. Consider, for example, the concept of acquiring knowledge to better one's self. In approximately 370 B.C., a great library was built in Alexandria, Egypt, an edifice which represented the acquired knowledge of mankind (up to that time), and which had little or nothing to do with money. It contained the works of Plato, Aristotle, Euclid and all of the other great intellectuals of that time. – up to 700,000 manuscripts, all housed in ancient splendor.[2] Imagine a society spending that much time and money on knowledge, creating one of the Seven Wonders of the Ancient World, and it had nothing to do with money! Remember this the next time your community votes on whether to float bonds to build a new library.

Presumably, if Paul and his dad had ruled in ancient times, the shelves of the Great Library of Alexandria would have been loaded with currency, coins and bars of gold, not books. Could there be a better example of our shifting values?

---

[2] Hannam, James, *"The Mysterious Fate Of The Great Library At Alexandria,"* Bede's Library, 2003.

2. In the quest for money and wealth, anything goes. <u>Anything.</u>

Because we seemingly value wealth above all else these days, we are willing to do virtually **anything** to achieve it. And that means **anything.**

Crime and jail time? Check. Michael Milken, Martha Stewart, Joe Nacchio, and many other white collar executives have emerged from jail with a good portion of their fortunes largely intact. A few years in jail is but a small price to pay to emerge filthy rich. Nacchio was given a rather stiff sentence of six years in jail, $19 million in fines, and was forced to forfeit $52 million in earnings for defrauding investors – but will still emerge with more than $70 million in wealth from his five years atop Qwest Communications.[3] (His case is currently pending appeal after his conviction.)

> *"I'd go to jail tonight if I could get out a rich man tomorrow."*
> —Ned, 34, Business Owner, Roanoke, VA

The lottery? Check. Americans spend $25 billion per year on the lottery, and $90 billion per year in gambling emporiums from Las Vegas to Peoria.[4] The odds are staggeringly long and nearly impossible that anyone can win big, but many Americans **still** think they are going to beat them. We routinely find people in our focus groups that not only play the lottery, but do so as part of their financial "regimen." Never mind that they might be better off rolling their money and smoking it; how else could they get filthy rich except through the lottery?

---

[3] McGhee , Tom, and Vuong, Andy, *"Nacchio To Prison For Six Years,"* The Denver Post, July 28, 2007.
[4] Flynn, Sean, *"Is Gambling Good For America?"* Parade Magazine, May 20, 2007.

"I play the lottery every week. I know that eventually I'm gonna win big. And I mean big."
—Yaphet, 26, Unemployed, Richmond, VA

Real estate? Check. If TV is a reflection of culture, then real estate is a major source for building wealth. Turn on the tube on a given weekend and you'll see. . .how to "flip" houses (buy them just so you can sell them at a fat profit after adding a coat of paint and a few other "fix ups"), how to redecorate your house to maximize its sales value, infomercials on buying real estate without cash...heck, even shows where a stranger lives in your house and redecorates it while you're gone. (Who wouldn't want a stranger living in their house, changing all the furniture? Now **that's** an American Dream.) Many Americans are convinced that the road to a solid financial future runs straight through real estate.

"Real estate is the only real way to build wealth, if you ask me."
—Tad, 68, Retired, Madison, WI

"Everyone knows that the richest people in this country made all their money on real estate."
—Esteban, 58, Distributor, New York City.

Become CEO and raid the company treasury? Check. One of the easiest paths to wealth is to become a senior manager of an American company, even a struggling, unprofitable firm. While the aforementioned Joe Nacchio presided over the decline of Qwest to the point that the company was almost bankrupted, he pocketed more than $150 million in compensation during his tenure at the top.[5] Glenn Tilton of United Airlines was paid nearly $40 million as CEO in 2006, after just **one** profitable quarter since the airline had emerged from its 2002 bankruptcy

---

[5] McGhee , Tom, and Vuong, Andy, *"Nacchio To Prison For Six Years,"* The Denver Post, July 28, 2007.

26

filing.[6] Neither executive founded the company (was an owner-operator), risked their family fortunes to launch the company, nor will be hailed in the annals of American business as one of the all-time great innovators. All they did to earn their princely sums was to put three small letters on their business card – "C.E.O." And they're far from the only senior executives who've been richly compensated in recent times. The favorite two words in the executive suites these days are "stock" and "options."

But because Americans are so invested in wealth building, there is practically no limit to the things we'll try (and often fail at) in our quest to build vast riches. Prior to the tech bust of the late 1990's, many Americans felt that the **stock market** was the road to riches, until it tanked for nearly five years. But stock market losses hardly curtailed Americans' unquenched thirst for becoming filthy rich. No, if you scan infomercials on a Sunday morning (and really want insight into our culture and values), you'll see programs in recent months on **real estate, selling household junk on eBay, time share condominiums, day trading, and even how to make a fortune on...burial plots.** When it comes to money-making schemes, Americans are in a class by themselves these days.

Some of the poster children at the beginning of this chapter have been particularly creative when it comes to building wealth. Suzanne Mullins won $4.2 million in the 1993 Virginia Lottery, and then promptly borrowed almost $200,000 from the lottery against future earnings. (She later filed bankruptcy, keeping her winnings **and** the borrowed money![7]) Joe Francis has earned millions shooting nude videos of young girls on spring break – he's the creator of the "Girls Of..." series. Alas, Francis has run afoul of the law for tax evasion, but his videos are still marketed on infomercials during the wee hours of the night, and Francis jetted

---

[6] From the web site, Financialservices.house.gov.
[7] Goodstein, Ellen, "*Unlucky Lottery Winners Who Lost Their Money,*" Bankrate.com.

around the country on his private jet before heading to jail. (No, you can't see anything on TV, so don't bother staying up for the infomercials!)

But the Grand Prize for doing literally anything to succeed in life must go the Steinmetz High School Academic Decathlon Team. These high school students showed incredible pluck and bad judgment on their path to fame and fortune. Under the guidance of Dr. Gerald Plecki, who was "in" on the scam, they lost the 1995 regional Academic Decathlon in the Chicago area. But remember the New American Dream – do **whatever** it takes – and they did! The students somehow obtained answers to the academic exercises (they supposedly paid for the answers) and improved their scores by a miraculous degree, claiming the first state championship in school history. For a time, they became Chicago-area legends, with scholarships to college and other opportunities there for the taking. Alas, eventually they were caught and forfeited their prizes, achieving fame and fortune of a different sort.[8]

---

[8] From Wikipedia's online encyclopedia.

3.   *Americans want to build wealth <u>right</u> <u>now!</u>*

Not tomorrow, but now!

The Old American Dream involved attaining prosperity over time, usually a lifetime. Saving, investing, the appreciation in home prices, and building a pension were all considered **lifelong pursuits** that would lead to prosperity during our Golden Years. But no more. We Americans want money – and lots of it – **now**!

That's why we play the lottery, flip houses, commit crimes and even come home from the baseball game with some free trinket which we immediately post on eBay; it's all about making as much money as we can **right now.** (After the 1998 Major League Baseball All-Star game in Denver, hundreds of fans posted the free beanie baby given to them upon entering the stadium, selling them for as much as $500 the next day. So much for sentimentality and keepsakes from a big event.)

"I don't want to wait until I'm old to get rich. I want to live a little right now, while I'm young."
—Marla, 45, Secretary, Greenwood Village, CO

"I'll do whatever it takes to make my money as fast as I can."
—Rafael, 23, Student, Oakland, CA

"Sometimes you have to cheat at work to get ahead. That's just the way it is. Otherwise, it just takes too long until you're rich."
—Rich, 30, Middle Manager, Sacramento, CA

"I feel that I have a better chance of winning the lottery than I do of getting ahead at work. If you work hard, you get screwed. It's all about politics and a— kissing."
—Bernice, 53, Office Worker, Overland Park, KS

Our drive to maximize wealth in the near-term, or for immediate gratification, is so strong that we can now trace a cycle of wealth-building scams, crises and economic downturns over the past twenty years, as waves of Americans were overcome with greed and couldn't help but "go for the gold."

- **The S & L Scandal** – In the mid to late 1980's, the federal government had to pay out billions of dollars to cover the losses of Savings & Loans which had given out billions of dollars under the guise of business "loans." Not surprisingly, the money was lost for good, and taxpayers and depositors had to foot the bill, while a few Americans made out like bandits.

- **The Tech Stock Boom** – Remember all the "paper millionaires" in the late 1990's who quit their day jobs to go off to an Internet firm, in search of stock options and instant wealth? Some made fortunes, but many were burned when these profitless, revenue-less companies bit the dust.

- **Day Traders** – For a time near the turn of the century, we swallowed the urban legend that you could make millions by trading stocks relentlessly while wearing your bedroom slippers and robe at home. We know better now – most "day traders" had to get day jobs to pay off their debts.

- **Flip This!** – For a time in the early 2000's, there were more than a few shows on cable which featured house "flippers" who made millions buying and selling properties. They made it seem as easy as "1-2-3," and you could reap millions by painting and wallpapering run-down properties. The reality was that many "flippers" in Nevada, Florida, California and other "hot" real estate markets were burned; one man's trash isn't always another's gold.

- **<u>Mortgage/Credit Crunch</u>** – Having failed to make money in the stock market, many turned to an overheated real estate market in 2006 and 2007. Vast wealth was just an "adjustable mortgage" or "mega mortgage" away. Home prices would always rise, wouldn't they? Alas, like all of the other get-rich-quick schemes noted here, real estate gains were "fool's gold" for many – by the Fall of 2007, delinquencies and foreclosures had hit an all-time high as a spate of mortgage firms, and consumers, went belly-up.

"It's like Governor Schwarzenegger says. It's just so easy to get rich in this country."
—D'Andre, 25, Entrepreneur, Los Angeles, CA

<u>Why The Dream Changed</u>

Our grand American experiment with democracy has been an unquestioned success. The United States is a political, economic and military superpower that has reached extraordinary heights in the last hundred years, from the liberation of Europe to landing a spacecraft on the moon. That's not to say that the ride over the past two hundred thirty years hasn't been bumpy at times (recall The Civil War...The Great Depression...Vietnam). But it's difficult to imagine why we'd want to change The American Dream, given our success. After all, the Old American Dream served us so well for more than two hundred years.

"This is the greatest country on earth. No question about it."
—Aziz, 43, Retail, Atlanta, GA

"I think most Americans still think of us as a superpower. No other country on earth is like the U.S."
—Margo, 28, Account Executive, Shaker Heights, OH

Focus group sessions indicate that the American Dream hasn't changed because of any coordinated effort or conscious decision on the part of Americans. Rather, a number of factors have conspired to radically change the Dream in recent years.

First and foremost, focus groups indicate that the New Dream is motivated primarily by **greed.**

Greed is typically defined as a desire to acquire or possess more than what we need or deserve – and that's certainly what's driving the New American Dream. We simply want more and more money and material wealth, the sooner, the better. And we can never have enough, at least according to this New Dream.

Greed is eternal; it has always been a part of our society, and it always will – so why is greed only now rearing its ugly head in America? While greed certainly **could** have influenced the American Dream up to now, never have we lived in a time of such wealth and material abundance. As Charlotte Beyer of the Institute for Private Investors has noted, in somewhat of an understatement, "There has been an explosion of wealth in America."[9] The statistics don't lie – we are far richer than ever before, from the number of millionaires and billionaires to our per capita income. Accordingly, greed now runs rampant, and has swallowed up the American Dream. Greed is one of our Seven Deadly Sins, and its influence on the American Dream is unlikely to subside any time soon, or at least as long as our country is awash in material wealth.

---

[9] Pirto Heath, Rebecca, *""Life On Easy Street,"* American Demographics, April, 1997.

Beyond the exponential growth in our material wealth, several other factors are driving greed to the forefront of American life, and impacting our Dream. Focus group participants indicate that key factors include:

Beyond Greed...

Other Factors Impacting The Dream

1. **THE 1970'S ECONOMY**
2. **THE MEDIA**
3. **WE HATE WORK**
4. **GLORIFYING RETIREMENT**
5. **THE RISE OF THE FLOWER CHILDREN**

The 1970's Economy – For most of the country's history, we've been remarkably prosperous. Our work ethic, a largely free-market economy, and America's vast resources have combined to deliver an economic juggernaut. However, we've hit occasional rough patches, including a number of "Panics" (as downturns were called in the 1800's) and The Great Depression (from 1929 to 1941). Some readers may be too young to remember the broad economic malaise of the 1970's, which was often termed "stagflation" – in recognition of the economy's stagnant growth combined with rampant inflation. In addition, the economy was ravaged by high unemployment and high interest rates. True, the economy grew for most of the decade, but the ride was bumpy, indeed, to a generation that had known nothing but prosperity since The Great Depression.

Accordingly, many current middle-aged and older Americans tell us that they rationalize going for the gold because of this period of economic upheaval – i.e., they **never** want to struggle again like they did in the 1970's.

"When I was young, the economy was really rough, and I swore that I my family would never be at risk again. So making sure we have financial security is a major priority."
—Corey, 40, Executive, Loveland, CO

"Things are so much better now than in the '70's. I sure hope they stay that way."
—Banton, 46, Postal Carrier, Dearborn, MI

The Media – We seem to blame the media for **everything**. But in this case, it's warranted. The media's focus on wealth, and the benefits of wealthy lifestyles has certainly helped to alter our value system, and the Dream.

"Everything you see and hear is about how great money is. And they're right. Money is great."
—Shane, 16, High School Student, Mesa, AZ

In the 1980's, we envied Robin Leach's *Lifestyles Of The Rich & Famous* – who wouldn't want to eat caviar, fly around the world on a Learjet, and wake each morning to the sounds of the Pacific Ocean crashing ashore? But our interest in material wealth has only intensified since then.

On reality shows like *Survivor* and *Big Brother*, contestants duel for million-dollar prizes through treachery, deceit, backstabbing, and manipulation of fellow contestants, a perfect allegory for our modern American Dream. And game shows like *Who Wants To Be A Millionaire?*, *Deal or No Deal* and *Power of 10* also reflect our New

Dream, as contestants don't just compete for the old standard "cash and prizes," but for **mega-cash** payouts of $10 million or more.

> *"I think that's the American Dream to compete for a million bucks like they do on 'Survivor.'"*
> —Zane, 22, Student, Irving, TX

> *"On TV, everyone seems rich."*
> —Melody, 24, Clerk, Manchester, MO

But that's just TV, the proverbial "boob tube." Certainly, other media reflect more than just a primordial urge for wealth and material goods, right? Well, in 2006 and 2007, bestsellers included *The Millionaire Next Door, Rich Dad, Poor Dad*, and, in the interest of variety, *Millionaire Women Next Door.* (Emphasis added.)

Of course, the New American Dream isn't just for adults. Teens can tune into MTV's *Cribs* or *Sweet 16* to understand the importance of money, wealth and power, even for young kids just learning to drive. Or they can even tune into MTV's *The Real World*, the original reality show, to show cast members living in such austere surroundings as the Vegas Strip, South Beach (Miami) or Sydney Harbour.

Perhaps the best evidence of the media's influence on our American Dream is the mysterious case of Donald Trump. What's mysterious about Trump is that he is totally lacking in charm, humor, grace, or inspiration; yet, he's somehow become an American icon. His one defining characteristic is simply that he's rich, and that's enough to make him a media star, in this era of the New Dream.

> *"I love Donald Trump. He is just so rich."*
> —Marcia, 44, Housewife, Redondo Beach, CA

We Hate Work — Despite polling data to the contrary at times, **most Americans are highly dissatisfied at work, according to our focus groups.** From pay to benefits to a lack of respect from co-workers, Americans complain loudly and vociferously about how much – or how little – they enjoy work these days.

This dissatisfaction with work has spawned an interest in…**not** working. Whether through retirement or simply striking it rich (remember the lottery?), Americans would prefer not to live to work, but to live to live.

Consequently, our dissatisfaction with working life drives our interest in vast sums of wealth – the more money we have, the less likely we are to need to work.

"I pray that I can hit the lottery and get out of my miserable job."
—Juan, 44, Account Executive, Des Plaines, IL

"If I didn't need the money, there is no way I would work."
—Bo, 32, Retail, Cleveland, OH

"I want to be a millionaire, so that I don't ever have to work."
—Al, 12, Student, Louisville, KY

Glorifying Retirement — Beyond hating work, retirement has been subtly repositioned during the last twenty years or so, from a time where the aged cease to be functional, to a pure celebration of life.

Once, retirement was an aimless time of discontent, when Americans rued their lack of usefulness to society and were largely waiting to die. It was a purgatory of sorts.

But in the last twenty years, the financial services industry (mainly, the purveyors of retirement plans) and the health care industry (vitamins and prescription drug makers) have portrayed retirements in their marketing campaigns as a Valhalla of sorts. They picture retirement as a time for living lavishly in dream homes, for hyperactivity as we run marathons and swim the channel (despite having false teeth and numerous other age-related maladies), and for absolutely unlimited fun with parties, dinners, celebrations and more. Why, nobody **ever** seems to be having a bad time in retirement; in fact, it really does seem like nirvana. (We suppose that this is what heaven used to seem like in the minds of many Americans.)

As a consequence, the concept of **early retirement** has spread like wildfire. What age do you want to retire at? Like an infomercial, the answer is low, lower, or lowest. Sixty-five? No way. Do I hear fifty-five? Forty-five? Gulp, Forty?

Of course, to retire this young, we'll need plenty of money, and sooner, much sooner, than later. Hence, our need for a New American Dream.

The proliferation of financial planners for retirement has forever changed our views on money. No longer content simply to live well and save our money as we earn it, now we must **maximize** our yield on numerous investments, right here, right now. Thus, we look for our homes to appreciate, for our stock funds to out-gain the S & P 500, and for various IRA's and retirement funds to gain at least 10% per year. As a society, we simply fixate on money. We no longer measure the worth of a man by his contributions to society, how well he parented, or the strength of his character – but, rather by his net worth.

The Rise Of The Flower Children – We've identified a very unique pattern with respect to acquiring wealth in our focus groups. Those respondents (participants in the group) who claim to have been "hippies" or "flower children" are now most desirous of acquiring wealth and material possessions, and doing literally anything to become wealthy.

We theorize that these Americans somehow feel that they missed out as youth, spending their time with drugs, free love and other accoutrements of the hippie lifestyle while their fellow Americans were out pursuing education, jobs, and, ultimately, money and material possessions. Hence, this group of "hippies" and "flower children" – literally, millions of Americans in their fifties and sixties – are helping to set the tone for America's values now that they're part of mainstream society once again.

The hippie mantra of the 1960's has been slightly amended: "Baby, tune in, turn on…and get rich!"

> *"I did an awful lot of drugs when I was young, really, everyone did… now I'm really into the stock market."*
> —Derrell, 61, Semi-Retired, Yorba Linda, CA

The Future

While we've never claimed to be seers or fortune-tellers, we don't foresee the factors sparking the change in the American Dream abating any time soon. Consequently, this new American Dream is likely to shape, and reshape, American life for at least several generations to come. So what changes has this New American Dream wrought?

1)   **Changes In Values** – Chicken or egg? Egg or chicken? What we mean is, did the New Dream spark changes in our values, or did our changing values impact the Dream? Based on what we've heard from thousands of Americans in our focus groups, it would appear to be a little of both.

The New Dream appears to have had a palpable impact on our core values as Americans. While the impact is intangible, and difficult to quantify, the New Dream appears, at a minimum, to have impacted our commitments to:

2)   **Honesty & Integrity** – Recall that the New Dream involves doing **whatever** it takes to acquire wealth. If you need to shade the truth a bit (or more than a bit), so be it. Author Ralph Keyes has written an entire book on this subject, dubbed ***The Post-Truth Era: Dishonesty & Deception In Contemporary Life***. Keyes goes so far as to boldly warn that, "Casual duplicity picks at the threads of our social fabric."

Our work tends to mirror Keyes'. We find that Americans **routinely** shade the truth (or lie) about a wide variety of subjects, including:

What Americans Fib About	
• Age	• Income
• Job Title	• Education
• Achievements of children	• Medical history/condition
• Sexual Activity/Proclivity	• Past Romantic Interests
• Knowledge of current events	• Size of their home(s)
• Attendance at events	• Vacations
• Amount of time spent on leisure activities	• Number of hours worked per week

This list is by no means complete – we would need to devote the whole book to the list in order to be thorough. Admittedly, most of these subjects are personal, in nature, and rather innocuous; lying about your children's achievements on the annual Christmas card is not terribly harmful.

Alas, many of our lies and mistruths can be quite harmful. Imagine lying about your family's income in order to receive college financial aid. One can imagine a full range of serious consequences from this "fib," from the government raising taxes to pay excessive aid, to a deserving family being denied aid due to shortfalls. Imagine the impact if you lie about the size of your house in order to lower your insurance rates; ultimately, most lies have tangible consequences.

3)   **Thriftiness** – Our national savings rates have hit historical lows; never have Americans saved as little as we do now. But as long as we count on stock options, winning the lottery, inventing the next "big thing" or some other windfall, we'll continue to show little interest in saving even a small amount that can turn into a big amount over time.

"I know I should save. But it's just so darn hard to find the money when there are so many other fun things I want to spend it on."
—Leon, 34, Delivery Driver, Missoula, MT

"My kids are young; I'll worry about paying for college when they get there."
—Jim, 35, Engineer, Fort Collins, CO

4)   **Hard Work** – We believe that one of the most tangible impacts of this New Dream is the distinct softening of the American work ethic. Why bother with hard work (manning a drill, driving a truck, or working 16-hour days in the office) when you can win the lottery, cheat on your taxes, flip houses, or pursue any other get-rich-quick scheme?

You wouldn't; hence, we Americans don't work nearly as hard as generations ago.

"Life's too short to spend so much time working."
—Severiano, 29, Unemployed, New York City

"I don't need to work that much. I'm sure that I will inherit a bundle some day."
—Delores, 30, Freelance Writer, Charlotte, NC

"Work? No way. I'm going to win the lottery, baby."
—Devon, 25, Student, Irwindale, CA

Other changes that this New American Dream has wrought include:

5)   **Rising White Collar Crime** – Crime simply doesn't pay. Oh wait, it does! Somewhat related to our declining values, we expect a steep uptick in white collar crime in coming years, as many Americans start to believe that the quickest way to wealth is simply to cheat.

As documented throughout this chapter, many American Dreamers plunder shareholders or the corporate treasury and emerge after a year or two in prison with their fortunes largely intact. Michael Milken, Martha Stewart, Ivan Boesky, and Jeffrey Skilling are but a few of the senior execs who've traded in pinstripes for even wider pinstripes in recent years. But that's not the only way to get a job making license plates in the Big House.

We expect in future years that more Americans will be guilty of illegal stock trades, income tax evasion, bank fraud, and other white collar crimes. This new Dream more often seems like a bad dream.

"Hell yes I'll go to jail if I can come out rich."
—Dale, 39, Engineer, Beaverton, CO

"It's worth it. You do the time for a bit, and these guys come out rich.
—Richard, 46, Banker, Bloomington, MN

6) **<u>Acute Labor Shortages</u>** – Americans are literally in love with the concept of retirement. Many aren't sure how much money they'll have (or whether it will be enough) and what they'll be doing, but they're absolutely sure they don't want to work during their Golden Years – far from it. Most Americans want to retire in their forties and fifties. Remember, the New American Dream isn't about work ethic and saving for a lifetime, but about striking it rich right now!

Accordingly, we expect at least some of the aging Baby Boom generation to leave the work force prematurely, especially senior white collar executives with access to stock options, golden parachutes and early retirement buy-outs. At a time when declining birth rates have already called into question our ability to staff the work force, early retirees may cause a "brain drain" in some industries or sectors of the economy – there simply won't be enough skilled white collar employees with extensive experience and know-how, especially in industries like financial services, travel and home building that pay giant bonuses to senior managers.

"Retiring early is my dream."
—Doris, 42, Secretary, Princeton, NJ

"I can't wait until I don't have to get up every day. It will be the best thing in the world just to relax."
—Carl, 56, Financial Services, West Covina, CA

"I don't know what I'm going to do when I retire. I just know I won't be working any more, and that will be great."
—Stephen, 41, Delivery Driver, Kenner, LA

7)   **Economic Boom-And-Bust Cycles** – Most readers are too young to remember the boom-and-bust nature of the American economy for most of the past century. The word "recession" struck fear into most Americans, with declining incomes and unemployment plaguing our economy every four to eight years, on average, followed by "boom" cycles. (We had twenty-one recessions in the 1900's, according to the National Bureau of Economic Research.)

However, since 1982, our economy has changed drastically. We've experienced a quarter century of economic growth, interrupted by only two minor recessions; they were considered minor due to their short duration and the comparatively mild contraction of the economy.

But we expect the swashbuckling nature of the New American Dream to reintroduce the "bust" cycle into the American economy. Recall the short list of economic downturns/crises we listed earlier in this chapter:

- **The S & L Scandal** (mid to late 1980's)
- **The Tech Stock Boom** (mid to late 1990's)
- **Day Traders** (late 1990's)
- **Flip This! (Real Estate)** (mid-2000's)
- **Mortgage/Credit Crunch** (2007)

This isn't an accident; in our quest to acquire gobs of money in the near-term, we'll try practically anything and take nearly any risk (and we have). Accordingly, from shady S & L loans to flimsy mortgages, each of the minor economic crises listed above was feared to have triggered an economic recession, and at least two of these crises were actually linked to the two mild recessions we experienced in the last twenty-five years.

We expect the number of "busts" to rise dramatically as we further pursue our New American Dream. Stocks, real estate, precious metals, insider trading, stock options, the lottery – this is the current recipe for the New American Dream. And with this recipe, there will be more financial scandals and risky ventures, key to the "bust" cycles.

Recap:
Future Impact Of The New Dream

> **Changes In Values**
  - **Honesty & Integrity**
  - **Thriftiness**
  - **Hard Work**

> **Rising White Collar Crime**

> **Acute Labor Shortages**

> **Economic Boom-And-Bust Cycles**

Conclusion

Think for a moment about the movie Independence Day. Gigantic alien aircraft hover over the White House, Wall Street, the Golden Gate Bridge and other key landmarks of American life, ready to strike violently at any time, and without warning. The alien aircraft have an almost paralyzing effect on American life in the movie – who can function normally with the mysterious alien gunships perched perilously close? The New American Dream is like those aircraft; it's casting a very large shadow over **every** aspect of our lives. Indeed the impact of the New American Dream will be documented throughout the coming chapters as we proceed on this journey across America.

Charles William Dement once remarked that, "Dreaming permits each and every one of us to be quietly insane every night of our lives." Or, in the case of this New American Dream, not just at night, but during the day, as well.

Chapter 2: Goodbye &

Good Riddance

☆ ☆ ☆ ☆ ☆

"I don't watch TV much any more, and I sure don't go to the movies. I've just figured out that there's a lot better ways to spend my time than when I was younger. I walk, go fishing, spend time with my wife. But not much TV and not many movies."
—J.T., 46, Construction Worker, Spokane, WA

"TV, radio, movies...it's all a bunch of crap these days. I miss the old days, you know, like classic TV, you know, like 'Silver Spoons' or 'Facts of Life.'"
—Joan, 36, Fashion Designer, New Rochelle, NY

The Call

"This is 9-1-1. What is the nature of your emergency?" the voice asked.

"Uh, he's dying."

"Sir?" the 911 operator asked again in a monotone. *"Please say again clearly. Do you have a crisis?"*

"Yes. I mean, he's flat-out dying."

"Yes, sir," the voice responded without emotion. *"We will send an ambulance and Emergency Services Team out immediately. What is the victim's, er, patient's, name and address?"* the voice asked flatly.

"It's, uh, it's, uh, it's Big Media," came the halting response, almost in disbelief.

"Are you sure of that?" the dispatcher asked.

"Yeah, that's right, Big Media," the despondent voice at the other end replied.

The Ambulance Ride

The back door slammed and the ambulance lurched forward, the siren blaring its primordial scream.

"This is EMT 0-7-8'er," a technician shouted into his microphone in the back of the ambulance. "Estimated arrival time," he continued while glancing at his watch, "is eleven minutes to ER. Copy. Eleven minutes."

"Roger that," a voice replied. "What are the symptoms of the patient?" the voice asked, too placid to suit the tastes of the EMT technician.

"What?

"What are the symptoms of the patient?" the dispatcher asked again, his voice now betraying a hint of irritation.

"Hey, I said I've only got eleven minutes 'til arrival – not an hour," the technician answered.

"What are the symptoms?" the flat voice asked again without emotion, dismissing the technician's misguided attempt at humor. "Repeat, what are the symptoms?"

"Well, then pull up a nice soft chair, partner, cause here we go. We don't have much time, but there's lots to talk about. Uh, well. I, uh. I guess I could start with...say, would you mind if I collect my thoughts for a moment and get right back to you? Copy?

"Copy," the voice at the other end responded almost immediately.

The technician began thinking...what had happened to Big Media, and why?

The Symptoms

Before you read on, it's natural to wonder, what is "Big Media" and, more importantly, why should you care about it? So before we get back to our patient, here's a brief explanation.

Big Media refers to the large corporations that own and operate **traditional** media outlets in the U.S. and worldwide. Traditional media includes:

- The major **broadcast networks** – like CBS, NBC and ABC.

- Major **daily newspapers**, from your local hometown rag to the Grey Lady (*The New York Times*).

- Major **cable networks** – like CNN, Fox and ESPN. (Yes, some of these networks pretend to be "new media," but most are owned by the very same media companies that own the major broadcast networks, like General Electric, Viacom, and Disney, to name a few. They are still "Big Media" in every way, shape and form.)

- Traditional **FM** and **AM radio stations**, like WCBS (New York), WBBM (Chicago), KCBS (Los Angeles), KMOX (St. Louis) and our personal favorite, KOA (Denver).

- Popular, high-circulation magazines, from *Sports Illustrated* to *TIME*.

- **Major movie studios**, from Paramount to 20th Century Fox, and the movies they produce and sometimes foist off on unsuspecting moviegoers.

In addition, "Big Media" usually refers to very large media companies that become an "empire" or conglomerate when multiple media combine under one group or parent company – i.e., Fox is not just your local affiliate, but a movie studio, a major broadcast network (home of *The Simpsons*), a cable news channel, and part of a media conglomerate that also owns numerous newspapers, including the prestigious *Times Of London,* among other properties. Other examples of Big Media "players," or the companies that own and operate vast media empires, include Disney (ABC, ESPN, Disney Studios), Time Warner (TIME Magazine, Time-Warner cable, TBS, AOL), and Viacom (MTV Networks, CBS).

Suffice it to say that the death of Big Media is **very** important to the average American, since Big Media has traditionally influenced everything from how we're entertained (recall the hours you spend each week channel surfing) to how we keep up with the world around us (the news). Why, Big Media has even supported many companies (our employers) through the years by selling literally billions of dollars worth of products via the ads carried in the media. Big Media has been an integral part of **all** of our lives for generations. Still not sure you should care about Big Media? Perhaps the best way to assess the impact or importance of Big Media on our lives is to imagine a world **without** Big Media – that is, **living your life without:**

- All of the TV you watch, from the daffy, tunnel-dwelling rodents of Meerkat Manor (on Animal Planet) to the even daffier, tunnel-dwelling residents (POW's, actually, some of whom resembled rodents) of the prison camps on (TV re-run) *Hogan's Heroes* – and **everything** in between.

- **The daily newspapers you read**, whether it's *The New York Times* or the *Wisconsin Rapids (Wisconsin) Daily Tribune* (the author's hometown rag growing up), which you use to keep up on sports, learn about life from "Dear Abby," read about all the bad news that's fit to print, and even use to line your favorite pet's cage.

- **All of the radio stations in your car.** That's right, without Big Media, there would be no traffic updates, no bad songs, and, worst (or best?) of all, no phone calls from dimwitted listeners to talk radio hosts, who ultimately make sport of, embarrass, and humiliate the caller.

- **All of the hit movies** produced by the major studios, from *Howard The Duck* to *Evan Almighty.* Okay, just kidding. Those weren't hits... were they? For every five bombs produced in Hollywood, there is probably an all-time classic like *Gone With The Wind* or *The Way We Were* that you just **have** to keep in your DVD collection. Hit movies cost hundreds of millions to produce these days, and without Big Media's deep pockets, you'd probably have to say goodbye to the local multi-plex.

- And without Big Media, you probably wouldn't be able to buy **hit CD's** (note to young readers, they used to be called albums) from the likes of The Eagles, The Beatles, or rapper Nas – or whatever musical acts float your boat. (See comment above on the cost of producing movies – the same applies to major musical acts.)

This is an abbreviated list. Suffice it to say, Big Media exerts a **major** influence on our lives, in many different ways, on a continuing basis. But more on the impact of Big Media later in this chapter. For now, let's get back to the symptoms of Big Media's demise.

While some readers may argue that Big Media remains healthy and vital (why, we all tune into *American Idol* with passion and fervor…at least most of us do), the symptoms of Big Media's impending doom are overwhelming. Perhaps the symptoms are so alarming that one might even surmise that Big Media isn't dying a slow, painful, old-age type of death, but something more akin to the spectacular flameout of a shooting star. In no particular order, chew on these symptoms:

- **Network TV ratings** plummeted to their lowest level ever in July of 2007 – and continue to fall. The audience for network TV is **less than half as big as it was in the 1980's.**[10] That's not a gradual erosion of audience, but an absolute tsunami, which has cost that industry **tens of billions of dollars** (that's not a typo) in advertising revenue. To put things in perspective, our country's population has grown by more than thirty million citizens since the 1980's, yet the audience for everything from the evening news to the top-rated network sitcom, is **down** significantly.

---

[10] BoingBoing, *"Worst Week in the History of Broadcast TV,"* Jul 21, 2006, and Anderson, Chris, *"Media Meltdown,"* August, 2006, A.C. Nielsen TV Report.

- **Radio ratings** (collectively) have plummeted for decades – and continued to fall by about 8% in 2006 from year-ago levels. By 2005, the average American listened to 11% fewer hours of radio per week,

- **Newspaper circulation peaked in 1987** – and continues to fall. In all, circulation was off by approximately 3% last year, and down more than 15% since 1985, despite the fact that there are at least thirty million more Americans than in 1985.[11] Employment in the newspaper industry has fallen 18% between 1990 and 2004.

- DVD sales – supposedly a "new media" format of our beloved movies and TV, were off 3% to 4% in 2006.[12]

- Hollywood just ain't what it used to be. Box office ticket sales have declined since reaching a peak for the modern era in 2002.[13] (Ticket sales actually peaked in the 1940's, when films were mostly black-and-white, and the idea of an R-rated movie was merely a glimmer in a producer's eye.)

- **Newsstand sales of magazines have hit an all-time low**, at least since sales have been tracked by Madison Avenue.[14]

---

[11] *"Newspaper Audience Average Circulation of U.S. Daily Newspaper,"* State of the News Media 2007 -The Project for Excellence in Journalism, Copyright 2007.
[12] Thomas, Arnold, *"Summer Blockbusters Boost Holiday DVD Sales,"* The Hollywood Reporter, Arnold Thomas, July 17, 2007
[13] *"Total U.S Theatre Admissions,"* National Association of Theatre Owners (NATO), Copyright 2007,
[14] Anderson, Chris, *"Media Meltdown,"* August, 2006

- Sales of CD's and cassettes (for major music acts) are off by 21% since their peak in 1999 – and an astounding 15% in the first six months of 2007.[15]

Clearly, the steep downturn in the fortunes of Big Media is neither short-term in nature, nor a minor dip in Big Media's outlook. Instead, we are seeing, quite literally, the death of Big Media as we know it. The media landscape is changing radically, and at a rapid pace. Big Media isn't hanging on, but is receding from our lives faster than Al Gore thinks our polar ice caps are melting. To say that Big Media is dying may be an **under**statement.

The Autopsy

"Scalpel please, doctor."

"Scalpel," the woman confirmed while slapping it into the palm of the coroner, as they both huddled over the dimly lit table, in a room so quiet, even a pin dropping might have wakened the dead.

"Bonesaw" the coroner continued.

After a few hacks with the saw, the doctor exclaimed, "Why, that's amazing."

"Yes, sir," the woman responded while jotting notes. "What's amazing, sir?"

"The deceased, er...Big, uh, Media," he said, almost spitting out the name, "has no heart."

What?"

"I repeat," the coroner said, "the deceased had no heart."

"That's not so amazing, doctor," the young woman, his assistant, responded earnestly, if not breathlessly. "Everyone already knew that Big Media was heartless."

---

[15] Anderson, Chris, "The Long Tail," A.C. Nielsen Soundscan.

"Let's continue on. Please take precise notes," the coroner said. "Skull chisel," he announced, a large grin creasing his face…

Why have TV and radio ratings, movie ticket and book sales, newspaper circulation and CD/DVD sales all declined precipitously in recent years? The reasons for the demise of Big Media are as diverse as the media empires themselves, according to our focus group respondents.

WHY BIG MEDIA IS DYING

1. **BIG MEDIA'S OBSESSION WITH YOUTH.**
2. **THE DECLINING QUALITY OF BIG MEDIA.**
3. **CONSUMERS ARE TUNING OUT THE MEDIA.**
4. **TOO MANY ADS.**
5. **THE MEDIA IS OUT OF TOUCH.**
6. **CREDIBILITY PROBLEMS.**

Big Media's Obsession With Youth — Are you between the ages of eighteen and thirty-four? If so, congratulations – TV, radio and the rest of Big Media are designed for **you.** (At least they are, in theory. If we were that age, we're not sure that we would want to own up to movies like ***The Hills Have Eyes*** or some of the gangsta (c)rap turned out these days.) Not between the ages of eighteen and thirty-four? Well, sorry; you're just not welcome at the party. In other words, to Big Media, you don't exist.

American media is obsessed with youth, supposedly because young adults are more likely to try new brands/products and to adopt these brands/products as habits (become regular users), in comparison to older adults. Hence, Big Media designs its content for the youth market, hoping that advertisers will pay big money to reach their youthful audience by sponsoring a given show, movie, or other media property.

Alas, the strategy has been like a grenade that explodes in the face of Big Media, a self-inflicted wound. There are three main problems with Big Media's youth obsession:

1) **First, many readers, viewers, and listeners are simply turned off by Big Media, since it's no longer "age appropriate."** In basic terms, they simply hate the media content, because it's not designed for them. Think of it this way – you don't wear clothes made for a twenty-one year-old when you're almost seventy. You don't play with baby toys as an adult. So it's not surprising that:

   "Sitcoms on TV seem like they're made for young kids only. I just can't watch any more. I can't relate to the characters, and to be honest, I don't understand a lot of the dialogue. I feel like a dinosaur."
   —Annabel, 52, Retired, Davie, FL

   "Movies are all about sex and heat for kids. I just don't bother to go to the theater any more. It's a waste of time."
   —Gary, 49, Accountant, Belleville, IL

2) **The second major flaw with the youth strategy is that it's simply bad business** – marketers are focusing on a small minority of the U.S. population, at the expense of larger, more lucrative (and affluent) audiences. According to the U.S. Census Bureau, just 23% of the population is between the ages of eighteen and thirty-four. By comparison, about 40% of our country is between the ages of thirty-five and sixty-four. Worse, Age Wave, a San Francisco-based marketing consulting firm

estimates that consumers over the age of fifty represent **half** of all the discretionary spending income in the United States.[16] In essence, advertisers and Big Media are skipping over a big portion of the population, a group with money to burn.

"If a company doesn't want my money because I'm older, screw them."
—Juan, 61, City Maintenance, Pasadena, CA

"Quite honestly, I feel left out."
—Gary, 38, Small Business Owner, Plano, TX

3)   **Third, the theory which underlies Big Media's focus on youth is simply flawed, flat-out wrong.** If there is anything we can be sure of after thousands of focus groups over the past twenty-five years, it's that people of all ages will try and adopt new products, not just young adults. The idea that American consumers are "locked in" to brand choices as young adults is simplistic, at best, stupid at worst. While it's true that older adults are more habituated and less likely to adopt radical change, it's also true that we frequently change purchase patterns over the course of our adult lifetimes – a good product usually trumps our being stuck in a middle-aged or old-aged rut. We have literally thousands of quotes to illustrate that consumers above and beyond eighteen to thirty-four year-olds will try new products, change old habits, and adopt new products. But the quote below says it succinctly:

---

[16] La Monica, Paul R., *"Golden Oldies: Are Media And Entertainment Companies Understanding The Spending Power of Baby Boomers?"* CNN Money.com.

"Of course I'd try that. I don't care how old you are. If it's good, it's good. Age has nothing to do with that."
—Sindee Lew, 45, High School Gym Teacher, Jackson, MS

The Quality of Big Media Is Declining - Continuing our autopsy of Big Media, it's clear that declining usage of Big Media by consumers is also due, at least in part, to the diminished quality of media content. In a word often used in our focus groups to describe various media products and services, consumers believe that the media "stinks." What are the most frequent complaints about the quality of the media that we hear in focus groups?

Frequent Consumer Complaints
About The Quality Of Media

➢ Movies are loaded with special effects, at the expense of dialogue and scripts, which are just plain bad.

➢ Sitcom jokes are written for a very young audience – the jokes aren't natural or funny – they are simply "laugh lines" bolstered by artificial applause.

➢ Rap music? Are you kidding? That's an oxymoron. What happened to classic rock, Motown, soft rock…

➢ There's too much sex and violence on TV.

➢ There's too much sex and violence at the movies.

➢ Newspapers suffer from liberal bias.

➢ Who has time to read a newspaper in the morning?

➢ There is little originality in Hollywood or on TV – most shows are formulaic, sequels, or new versions of old concepts.

On those few occasions when Big Media **does** deliver quality, the rewards are rich, indeed. As evidence, consider *The Sopranos*, or the madcap comedy of *Seinfeld*, or even the residuals generated by *I Love Lucy* fifty years after it first ran on TV. (*Seinfeld* and *I Love Lucy* were named by *TV Guide* as the top two comedies of all-time several years ago.)

We're Tuning Out The Media - Consumers in focus groups indicate that they are paying far less attention to Big Media, in part, because they're simply overwhelmed with media content – that is, we Americans are **over stimulated**.

> *"I just get sick of watching the news, hearing the news, reading the news. It's depressing. And there are times when I just want to tune it out and get on with my life, if you know what I mean? Everywhere I look, it's news, news, news."*
> —Whitney, 34, Cashier, Kansas City, MO

> *"TV, the movies, You Tube, DVD's, where does it end? I don't think my kids know how to read a book. They just watch life, instead of reading or thinking about it. Or living it. It's like, the media IS life. And that's not right, at all."*
> —Audrey, 36, Housewife, Minnetonka, MN

In the 1950's, Americans primarily depended upon a daily newspaper, their radio and, to a lesser extent, their newfangled TV's to keep in touch with the world. We spent about an hour a day on Big Media, with the remainder of our time devoted to dinner with the family, long walks, and the comfort of a good book – you **do** remember those activities, don't you? Big Media was emerging, but it hadn't yet overwhelmed our lives.

Flash to the 2000's. Big Media is **everywhere**. Now, we have online media content (that we can access any time on our computers), cell phones, pagers, Blackberry's, iPods, and iPhones, . And we aren't just stimulated by what we read, but also by what we hear and see. TV's blare everywhere, from the doctor's office waiting room to the main aisle of our favorite department store, as well as for an average of eight hours per day in every American household. Cell phones ring indiscriminately, any time, any where. (The more annoying and obnoxious the ring, the more likely they are to ring – or so it seems.)

We have music and TV's in our elevators, on airlines, and even in many funeral parlors – ostensibly so the dead can stay "plugged in?" We can't get away from the media even when we're away (or dead). Travelers can stay in touch with the world through their cell phones, in-room Internet services, computers in Business Centers, FAX communications delivered to their rooms, and even through the good ol' color TV in each room.

And it's not just the number of opportunities to tap into Big Media that has increased through new devices. The sheer **volume** of Big Media **content** has literally exploded with gains in technology.

> *"It's like a horror movie with a creeping crud that keeps*
> *expanding and swallowing us up.. Every where you turn, there's*
> *a TV, a computer, a video, a radio. You can never just sit in*
> *silence any more. God forbid that you would."*
> —Jon, 37, Executive, West Chester, PA

Take just one example of Big Media – the radio – to see how content is exploding at a frightening pace. Once upon a time, we could tap into ten to twenty stations in major markets, perhaps three or four stations (if you were lucky) in small towns. We usually knew which stations were news and talk, and which stations were Top 40 Rock. Now, in addition to our own CD's and cassettes, we can also listen to music we've downloaded on our iPods or other devices. And if you're not content with programming your own radio station, flip on satellite radio, hundreds of channels of the most inane drivel imaginable, in many cases. (We particularly enjoy the Elvis channel which broadcasts from outside of The King's old Graceland mansion, twenty-four hours a day, seven days a week.) And some consumers actually pay extra to get all of these stations they've never listened to, and likely, never will, on satellite radio.

So how do our focus group respondents around the USA tell us that they're responding to the explosion in media content? By spending more time with media? By paying more attention to media content? Nope. They simply tune it out.

"When I was a kid, I watched TV all the time. Now, I mostly spend time in the garden or reading a good book."
—Dave, 48, Teacher, Longmont, CO

"I just get so sick of noise – Voicemail, radio, cell phones, Blackberry, e-mail, the Internet. You name it. So I find myself just sitting outside quietly, watching the sunset. To hell with that other stuff."
—Don, 39, Business Owner, West Valley, UT

Too Many Ads – T. S. Eliot was wrong. The world won't end with a bang, but with an ad. Or a bunch of ads.

If you've ever complained that there are too many ads on TV and the radio, you're not alone. Our focus group respondents are extremely disenchanted with the commercialization of Big Media.

"It's just about to the point that the ads take up more of the nightly news than the news itself. Really. I'm serious about that...
—Emily, 18, Student, Hialeah, FL

"I can't believe the number of ads on during football games, or even movies. It's staggering. I have trouble following the game or the movie these days."
—Brent, 23, Grocery Clerk, Dunedin, FL

And how are people responding to the ever-increasing onslaught of ads? They are simply losing interest in Big Media. But not just the ads. No, they throw the baby out with the bath water, turning out media content while dodging ads.

"My hand actually hurts from working the remote. I just won't watch ads when I'm watching TV. There's just too many of them."
—Holly Anne, 28, Housewife, Los Angeles, CA

"I flip from radio station to radio station, trying to avoid commercials, when I'm driving to work. And if there are too many ads, I just turn it off [the radio]."
—Pauline, 42, Secretary, Redondo Beach, CA

You don't need to be Sherlock Holmes or a Phi Beta Kappa to figure out why the media is increasing the number of ads carried on content. It's greed, pure greed. The more ads they run, the more money they make. In fact, despite the declining ratings and sales we highlighted earlier in this chapter, most major Big Media properties have increased their profits in the past two decades. Guess how? That's right, by simply running **more** ads.

Numerous national studies have documented the increase in ads. When TV was launched, the sponsor might merit a mention at the beginning or end of a program. That was the extent of the advertising. But no more. In the Spring of 2007, several media outlets highlighted that ABC is the most commercially oriented of the major broadcast networks, running more than fifteen minutes of ads per hour.[17] (MTV led all networks, with more than sixteen minutes of ads per hour.) If you're doing the math at home, that's one out of every four minutes that is an ad. And one out of every three minutes on each evening's newscasts is an ad.

---

[17] Salzman, Jason, *"Should Democratic Leaders Be So Cozy With Rosen?""* Denver Rocky Mountain News, April 14, 2007.

If you're thinking that radio is nearly as bad, it is. In the Denver market, where the author resides, the highest rated talk radio programs feature fifteen minutes of ads per hour, according to a report.[18]

With this penchant for running ads, Big Media isn't building long-term profitability. No, like a drug addict, it's simply fueling its own demise, a dependency on running more and more ads to offset declines in revenue caused by lousy content and all of the other problems noted in this chapter.

When the amount of advertising grows by such exponential proportions, viewers or listeners ultimately turn away. The more they turn away, the lower the ratings, which ultimately lowers the ad rates (or what Big Media charges advertisers to run ads), and forces Big Media to carry **even more ads** (which the media deems as "clutter.")

On top of that, when consumers are overwhelmed with ads, they tend to tune them out. They hear or see them, but they really don't "hear" or "see" them. So the ads are less effective, and advertisers eventually look for other places to spend their money.

It becomes, literally, a vicious cycle, a spiral downward for Big Media, as the media companies need more ads to stay financially viable, while advertisers become more and more disenchanted with the advertising vehicles. Soon enough, the system will break down.

"I can't remember a single ad I've seen recently. Not one. I just don't pay attention. They are too boring."
—Mel, 34, English Teacher, Norwalk, CT

"I know I heard some ads on the radio on the way over here, but I'm damned if I can remember what they were, who they were for, or what they said. In one ear, out the next, if you know what I mean."
—Genteel, 22, Aspiring Rap Artist, Atlanta, GA

---

[18] Salzman, Jason, *"Should Democratic Leaders Be So Cozy With Rose?"* Denver Rocky Mountain News, April 14, 2007.

The Media's Out Of Touch — Big Media is a bit like the late comedian John Belushi, at least when it comes to autopsies. The health of the deceased is so bad, the causes of death are so numerous that it's difficult to pinpoint just a single reason for Big Media's demise. So the list grows ever longer…

The use of Big Media is declining rapidly as it becomes ever more out of touch with the vast majority of Americans, especially those in the middle of the country, between the coasts. Quite naturally, we call this **"coastal bias."**

Americans in our focus groups claim that there is a significant bias in favor of the coasts – specifically, Southern California and New York City – at the expense of the tastes and interests of the other two hundred fifty million people (approximately) living in the middle of the U.S. In short, they simply don't relate to much of Big Media's content.

In 2000, Major League baseball executives were puzzled when the Mets-Yankees World Series generated the lowest ratings (up to that time) in history. They'd expected record high ratings, since, surely, the whole world is interested in New York City, right? (They were puzzled again in the Summer of 2007 when the mini-series *The Bronx is Burning* bombed, too, as it focused on the exploits of the late 1970's New York Yankees.)

All of the morning news programs originate from Manhattan, with its skyscrapers, busy streets, and brownstones. These shows, like NBC's *Today*, even try to build a populist image by showing hundreds of electronic voyeurs in the streets peering into their morning studios each day, amidst the hustle and bustle of Gotham. Of course, network execs are oblivious to the fact that most Americans have never been to New York City, don't live in a brownstone, and don't cab to work. Consequently, our focus group respondents have told us for years that they don't care about New Yorkers lining the streets each morning – they feel little kinship to these poor souls.

Ironically, this "coastal bias" comes at a time when technology has almost rendered the originating location of Big Media content as inconsequential. If you have a satellite uplink, you could originate the evening newscasts from the Mojave Desert or the top of Mt. Rushmore. With a computer and an Internet connection, you could write an entire issue of **TIME** Magazine from the backwoods of Minnesota or the Louisiana Bayou. But to many Americans in our focus groups, it seems as if Big Media is unaware that there is anything West of the George Washington Bridge (in Manhattan) or East of Las Vegas.

All network programming originates on either coast, including all newscasts, **The Tonight Show** (with Jay Leno) and even syndicated fare like **Regis (Philbin) & Kelly (Ripa) Live**, but never from the middle of the country. Gritty dramas like **Law & Order** repeatedly portray the mean streets of New York, while only an occasional oddball show like **Murder She Wrote** or **Ed** are situated outside the Big Apple or L.A. Often, these oddball shows feature offbeat characters and peculiar lifestyles, like the power lawyer who moved home to take over a rundown bowling alley inhabited by a cast of crazies on **Ed.** According to our focus group respondents, these shows clearly belie a New Yorker's or Angelino's view of middle America – stilted, stereotyped, and just plain not interesting.

"Hollywood's just plain out of touch."
—Joe, 62, Semi-Retired, Ballwin, MO

"I'm so tired of watching cops run around the streets of New York. It was okay on Kojak in the '70's, but what has that got to do with my life?"
—Troy, 44, Trainer, Austin, TX

We are finding increasing numbers of focus group respondents complaining about the characters and storylines portrayed by Big Media: gangsta rappers, drug addicts, gay fashion and interior designers, and the ever-present hooker with the heart of gold (think Julia Roberts in *Pretty Woman*, among others). Viewers don't necessarily object to these characters and storylines, but feel that they've been **overdone**, at the expense of portraying **any** slice of life from the middle of the country. In other words, *Leave It To Beaver* and *The Brady Bunch have* been replaced by hookers and gay best friends on TV.

Perhaps the best example of Big Media being "out of touch" with mainstream America is the comedienne, Rosie O'Donnell. She was a lightning rod for dissent and criticism during her time on *The View* and remains so in our focus groups. Perhaps no public figure is so reviled.

> *"What a moron she (O'Donnell) is. I wouldn't mind if the terrorists attack her."*
> —Phil, 52, Plumber, Ontario, CA

We could fill an entire book with Ms. O'Donnell's outrageous quotes and comments from the past few years. (She'd make a **great** focus group respondent, at least if you were planning to write a book about focus groups.) She's compared American troops to terrorists, made many cutting comments about our sitting President, and even threatened to sneak into Donald Trump's house (he's her arch-enemy) and rub her fat belly on him. We're not kidding.

It's clear from our focus groups that Ms. O'Donnell only attracts viewers in much the same way that many viewers watch NASCAR or pro wrestling – to see the carnage after the crash. There is no love or respect for O'Donnell, and virtually no one was sorry to see her leave TV, at least in our focus groups.

But that's not the way that NBC saw things. At a network press briefing in Hollywood to drum up interest in its fall schedule for 2007, one of the new Co-Chairmen of NBC, Ben Silverman, said that his network would "love to be in business with Rosie O'Donnell." Out of touch with middle America? You make the call.[19]

"It's as if the writers [in Hollywood] don't even know that we're out here between L.A. and New York. We're the majority of the country, for God's sakes."
—Bernie, 52, Entrepreneur, Fort Wayne, IN

"They are so weird and out of touch (in Hollywood), and it's reflected in the movies and shows. You watch some of this stuff and think, 'What the hell were they thinking?' Then you watch the news or read the paper and you figure out pretty fast that they are just way out there, so out of touch."
—Laverne, 37, Computer Technician, Las Cruces, NM

And the major consequence of Big Media's coastal bias? You guessed it. Americans are simply tuning out Big Media with greater frequency and consistency. Coastal bias is just another reason that Big Media is on life support.

Credibility Problems — We see one last major cause of death for Big Media.

Yes, Virginia, there **is** liberal bias in Big Media. Okay, okay. Before half the readers (or more) slam this book down, toss it away, and complain about our bias, let us explain.

I once had a boss who was fond of telling me, "My perception is **your** reality," especially during performance appraisals.

The same can be said for consumers – what they perceive often **is** reality, or becomes reality, at least in their minds. In fact or reality, the perception might not be true. But because one perceives it to be true, it

---

[19] Ostrow, JoAnne, *"NBC Brass Explains Why Being No.4 Isn't So Bad,"* The Denver Post, July 17, 2007.

might as well be. And so it goes with the concept of "liberal bias." Is Big Media really slanted toward a liberal point of view? Does Big Media reflect largely the needs, viewpoints and interests of liberal Americans? Are most members of Big Media really Big Liberals? I'll let you make the call. Numerous other books and commentators have tackled the complex subject of liberal bias, so we aren't going to spend any time on whether it exists in this book.

But we **will** spend a bit of time discussing what Americans **perceive** to be true with respect to liberal bias. Whatever your point of view on whether liberal bias exists, what's indisputable is that focus group respondents all across the country have told us for a decade or more that liberal **bias in the media is real** and **palpable**. And because this is the common perception, it's become another very negative reality for Big Media.

> *"There's no question that the media is full of liberals, and they tell only their side of the story."*
> —Geri, 48, Child Care, Des Plaines, Ill

> *"Liberal bias? Shoot, absolutely in this country."*
> —LeVar, 28, Tool & Die, Sugarland, TX

> *"You take what the media says with a grain of salt, because you know it's biased, toward the liberal point of view."*
> —Patrice, 42, Chef, Brookline, MA

Worse, the perception of liberal bias is deepening over the years. Perhaps a decade or more ago, most Americans in focus groups claimed that network news programs and their anchors, such as Dan Rather and Peter Jennings, were biased. Now, the belief is far more pervasive and deep. It's not just the news that's biased, but also news programs, documentaries, and even the entertainment content on the networks.

"That show 'Will & Grace.' Now tell me that wasn't the work of liberals to get a show to push the gay agenda on the air."
—Marcia, 44, Marketing, Menlo Park, CA

For newspapers, it was once just the editorial content that was labeled liberal. Now, it's the **entire** newspaper that's tinged with the "L" word, including news articles, business news and, most especially, the lifestyle sections of newspapers. Why, some of my focus group respondents even claim that the ads in newspapers are liberal, from the types of ads run (respondents always seem to recall ads for birth control, planned parenting, birth control remedies, and other liberal "causes") to the manner in which ads are presented, with racy pictures and coarse language.

"I can't believe the number of ads for strip clubs in the 'Dallas Morning News.' Now that's the work of liberal devils."
—John, 52, Consultant, Addison, TX

The same is true for the rest of the media. Cable content, with shows like *The L Word* (a lesbian ensemble drama) and *Big Love* (about a polygamist Mormon), is extremely liberal, at least according to some of our focus group participants. Radio shock jocks are morally bankrupt, obscene to many listeners (see Howard Stern), and the music played on the radio...need I say more? Well, it's probably worth noting that heavy metal and other types of traditionally "hard rock" music are often associated with Satanism... not exactly the preferred religion of mainstream America, and especially conservatives.

Even some of the newer entries from Big Media, like Microsoft/NBC's MSN division, one of the largest Internet providers and portals, has been cited as extremely liberal in our focus groups.

"Have you ever looked at the headlines they carry on MSN?
My God, they are so liberal, it's not even funny."
—Mary, 46, Medical Receptionist, Delafield, WI

"MSN's news coverage is consistently liberal."
—Marty, 49, Accountant, West Des Moines, IA

The net result of all this perceived – or real – liberal bias? Like all of the other symptoms listed at Big Media's autopsy, liberal bias has significantly enhanced the likelihood of individuals and households across the USA turning off, or tuning out, Big Media. ("Tuning out" means that it's still somewhat utilized, but its effect is greatly diminished by other media choices.) Until Big Media can address this credibility problem, millions of Americans will continue to tune it out, and seek alternative media sources, like Blogs, international newspapers, and the My Space web portal.

"I browse the Internet to get as many different sources as I can
for the news. That way, I'm not relying on one point of view
that's biased."
—Mychael, 26, Student, Vienna, VA

"I like to browse online for different newspapers, in order to get
a lot of different perspectives."
—Stacy, 37, Personal Trainer, Louisville, KY

"I keep up with the news on My Space, from what other people
have to say. I think it's a lot more reliable than our newspaper."
—Bobby, 59, Truck Driver, Enid, OK

The Future

Big Media isn't dead…at least not yet. Up to now, we've argued throughout this chapter that Big Media is near death, but it's not quite there, yet. Like a cancer patient, it's entirely possible that Big Media could retard its fundamental problems and prolong its useful life considerably, but only if Big Media takes drastic actions. It's also likely that consumers will increasingly respond to major changes in Big Media, as it lurches toward death, by changing how they use the media.

Over the years, I've documented how focus group respondents would like to see the media change, to make it more accessible, useful and credible. Our goal in sharing this is to give you, the reader, some sense of how Big Media might change (to the extent that it's customer focused) as it stumbles toward the "finish line" of its active life and takes its place in the heavens along with other deceased mega-products and services of the last century, such as the Edsel, hula-hoops, and 8-track tape players.

> *"When TV first came on, there was only one sponsor of a show. And you sure remembered who it was, and what they were pitching [selling]."*
> —Leo, 69, Retired, Scottsdale, AZ

The Return Of The Sponsored Show/Program: It's clear that the explosion in TV, radio, newspaper and magazine advertising has ultimately diminished the value and impact of ads, and destroyed the financial viability of Big Media. Need to pad the bottom line? Just add a few more minutes of advertising to your prime-time show. So what if the half-hour of TV or radio features 15 to 20 minutes in ads?

Clearly, the system's not working. No one remembers ads, viewers are just plain fatigued (or sickened) by the sheer volume of advertising, and the ads flat-out don't work at selling products and services. After all, you can't buy a product that you don't remember seeing or reading about. Companies continually reign in their media spending, fearing that the investment in ads is **not** paying off – and they're right!

Ultimately, we expect Big Media to return to its roots, the early days of TV and radio from the 1920's through the 1950's. The amount of advertising inventory will be **sharply reduced**, from fifteen minutes for every half-hour, to just a minute or two.

Advertisers won't run their ad twenty-five times in an evening. Instead, an ad will air just once per day, maybe as little as once a week. (Newspapers and magazines will significantly reduce the number of pages devoted to advertising.) In many cases, advertisers will sponsor an entire program (they will be the sole sponsor), earning the ensuing rights to broadcast their ad during the minute or two of advertising per hour. Imagine *American Idol, Sponsored By Columbia Records* or *CSI: Miami, Sponsored By The Florida Convention & Visitors Bureau*. There will be one – and only one – sponsor per half-hour or hour of TV and radio. Similarly, newspapers and magazines will carry ads by only a handful of key sponsors in each issue. (Imagine *reading The Chicago Tribune,* sponsored by Kraft.)

The result of this dramatic change? Viewers will stop changing the channels and dumping magazine and newspaper subscriptions, and will be deliriously happy that they can watch shows virtually uninterrupted, so media ratings (viewers, listeners, readers) should soar. The ads themselves will have far greater impact, as viewers will actually remember the names of sponsors and specific ads. The cost of ads will soar dramatically with the reduced inventory, but advertisers will be only too happy to pay as the public will actually see and remember their ads; in other words, companies will gladly pay for **high-impact advertising**. And by significantly curtailing the advertising inventory, Big Media will stimulate demand for limited ad spots; no longer will they have to sell ad space at a discount.

It is not overly dramatic to state that the sooner Big Media returns to its roots – i.e., the days of the sponsored show – the sooner it can forestall its seemingly inevitable demise. (It's inevitable with the current system.) However, starting this process will take courage from Big Media, and they still seem resistant to the idea of cutting inventory. But some smart media operators will figure this out soon enough; they will survive longer while other Big Media companies perish first. (For instance, the Howard Stern radio show limits its ad inventory, and limits when ads can be featured so as not to impact the viewing audience in a negative manner.)

Transforming Online Content To Mainstream Content: As Americans become increasingly disenchanted with Big Media, they've turned to alternative media such as blogs, satellite radio, and online video streaming services such as YouTube, and information and entertainment from Internet stations/networks like Mania TV.

To be fair, most of this "alternative" content is rubbish: poorly written, inaccurate, misinformed blog columns, stupid videos on YouTube with sub-standard production quality, and dull programming on satellite radio – is there really enough good music to program hundreds of radio "stations" to run simultaneously?

Despite the quality, there will be a winnowing out process with respect to alternative media. Some content **is** high quality, and will emerge as long-term media content. For instance, we'd expect that while our traditional newspapers offer online versions of their dailies, some online newspapers and magazines will go mainstream, and may eventually publish "hard" (paper) copies. We'd also expect that some YouTube content will become the "pilot" episodes for network TV of tomorrow, and perhaps, even become the newest broadcast network some day. (In 2007 and 2008, several Presidential debates featured questions submitted by YouTube users, via video.)

Changes In Ads: Today's ads simply don't work – there are too many of them, and, according to consumers, most ads simply aren't very good. In fact, most consumers tell me that ads are unwatchable or unlistenable. The multi-billion dollar economic system that's in place – where advertisers spend millions to reach consumers with messages through traditional media – won't survive if consumers continue to ignore most of the advertising they see and hear.

"I don't know how many times I've seen ads and tried to figure out what the hell they're selling."
—John, 81, Retired, Grosse Pointe Woods, MI

"There's [sic] too many ads. That's why I don't remember them."
—Sally, 29, Unemployed, Marietta, GA

Therefore, we expect most future ads to adopt one of the "high impact" styles of advertising that tends to grab consumers' attention in focus groups these days, based upon all of the ad testing we've done:

Star Endorsements: We are a celebrity-obsessed society, as will be discussed in more depth later in this book. Whether we want to admit it or not, when a major Hollywood star, TV star or musician tells us a product is good, we usually pay attention and listen, even if we don't always find the celebrity convincing. Celebrity is the "bully pulpit" of our society, according to our focus groups, even if the celebrity speaking to us is totally lacking in credibility, like Paris Hilton. (High-profile Hilton is a favorite target for criticism among focus group participants.) So we expect our advertisements to more closely resemble those of Japan and some other Far Eastern countries in the future – lots of glitz and Hollywood celebrities, and not much in the way of facts or information.

"I admit I bought the zit medicine when I saw Jessica Simpson [pitching it in TV ads]. I really love her."
—Amber, 15, Student, Mesa, AZ

*"I love Christie Brinkley's ad for Cover Girl. That's why
I buy it."*
—Amie, 38, Veterinary Assistant, Portland, OR

The Power Of Testimonials: Consumers respond very positively to testimonials, even from unknown, fictional "characters" in ads. But we make this assertion with two caveats, which ultimately impact the ad:

1) The more realistic the character(s) in the ad – up to, and including, using real people to give testimonials – the more believable and compelling the ad.

2) More factual testimonials have far more impact. In other words, telling me that nine out of ten doctors prefer a prescription drug is far superior to telling the public to use a drug simply because it works really well.

Ads That Tell A Story: Americans are clearly bored by contemporary ads. We don't watch most ads, don't remember them, and we certainly don't take much, if any, action in response to the ads. In other words, **contemporary ads don't work**. In many cases, it's simply because consumers have no idea what the ad is really all about – ads that are so "creative" that they are literally nonsensical to most viewers and readers. Think for a moment. When was the last time **you** watched an ad, and when it was done, your only response was, huh? What the heck was that? To most Americans, that's a daily occurrence.

In this environment, consumers tell us that ads which tell a distinct and compelling "story" of some sort are far more likely to be remembered, or to have an impact. Recall "Mikey" from Life cereal? Sure, it was a brief story. But most of us – at least those of us beyond a certain age – still remember that the cereal just had to be good if Mikey, the spoiled little child, loved it. Or how about the old woman (Clara Peller) who roared "Where's the beef?" in humorous vignettes for Wendy's, or even Apple Computer's Orwellian story in 1984 about the uniqueness of their new desktop computers? More recently, BMW has scored with ads that seem more like an action flick. We tend to remember holiday-themed ads for the same reason: – they usually tell a story of some sort about the holidays, and do more than merely pitch a product.

"I admit I logged onto BMW's site to follow up the ads. They were pretty romantic, all in all. The ads were just so great."
—Sara, 26, Housewife, Charlotte, NC

Free Sampling: It's not exactly the sexiest or most complex marketing ploy – you give away your product for free, in the hope that consumers will soon recognize the quality of the product and buy it at its regular price. Get used to it, because you're going to see it a lot more often in the future.

As consumers continue to tune out traditional advertising messages, marketers will increasingly rely on the product itself to make the sale. And if you can't give away a free product sample due to cost (like a car) or logistical problems (a house), then marketers will provide some type of sample that suggests the **essence** of the product, such as a free weekend (car rental) or a virtual tour in which the consumer can experience the product, while not actually using/buying it (a home).

"I love it when I can try the product. Then I know what it's all about. That's better than an advertisement, any time."
—Jason, 31, Sales Rep, Coconut Grove, FL

Fewer New Products: New products are particularly dependent upon advertising for success. Think for a moment about when you're new to a neighborhood or job. Somehow, you need to introduce yourself to your colleagues, or else you will remain isolated for an extended period of time. The same holds true for new products – from iPods to a new variation of your favorite dishwasher detergent – they must build awareness of the product and provide some rationale for why consumers should buy the new product. That's largely the role of advertising, which is the cheapest way to get the word out en masse.

However, since the impact of advertising is greatly diminished as Big Media is withering away, we're likely to see fewer successful new products launched in the near future. Can the world carry on without another new laundry detergent or another new hamburger at Burger King? Most definitely. But we also might miss the next iPhone or Xbox. And that would be a pity.

Non-Marketing Marketing: Our focus groups have indicated a distinct rise in what we've now termed as **"non-marketing marketing,"** because traditional marketing does not work and often irritates or offends potential buyers. At its most basic, non-marketing marketing is selling a product **without** really trying to sell it. Okay, okay, we realize this concept doesn't make much sense. But perhaps a few examples can best illustrate this concept.

What if your favorite movie featured a dress or a suit or a car that you couldn't get off your mind? Why, naturally, you **might** actually think about buying one – **that's** non-marketing marketing. The company would probably have paid to place their product in the movie (that's called product placement), knowing that some people might fall in love with the item. It's a conscious effort to market a product by **not** using traditional marketing methods, and definitely not using a "hard sell."

Other examples of non-marketing marketing? Background music on TV and at the movies, a software tutorial showing how other software programs could complement the software featured in the tutorial, or even travel videos on The Travel Channel featuring a specific airline or cruise ship. Ostensibly, all of these examples aren't the "hard sell," but information and entertainment…but we know that's not all they are.

"I still remember that song by Billy Vera & The Beaters on "Family Ties," that Michael J. Fox TV show. We all heard it on the show, and a few weeks later, it was Number One in the country. No one had ever heard of the song or Billy Vera. But it was just such a great song, and a great episode [of the show]."
—Eric, 40, Computer Repairs, Orange, NJ

A RECAP: THE FUTURE OF BIG MEDIA

➤ **The Return Of The Sponsored Show/Program**

➤ **Transforming Online Content To Mainstream Content**

➤ **Changes In Marketing Strategies:**
  - **Star Endorsements**
  - **The Power Of Testimonials**
  - **Ads That Tell A Story**
  - **Free Sampling**
  - **Fewer New Products**
  - **Non-Marketing Marketing**

The Eulogy

"And so, we now lay Big Media to rest," the priest said

*while looking out at the sparse congregation. He tried to imagine that the little old church was full, as it was much easier to preach if you felt you were **actually** reaching The Flock.*

"Big Media was, uh, Big Media was…around for a long time," he continued, spitting out the words. He stopped, unable to think of

anything else to say. After a brief pause while he composed himself, the priest continued, "Big Media provided many things to our society. We watched and heard and...we read Big Media nearly every day. Every day," he continued, as if that really mattered in the end.

The congregation shifted nervously in their seats, as if they'd rather be outside, at the mall, home... anywhere but the church as Big Media was being laid to rest.

"And so, I say to you," the priest bellowed, headed for a big finish, "Big Media will be remembered...uh, Big Media will be missed, uh... oh, to hell with it," the priest said, turning his back on the congregation. Like Big Media, he'd given up.

"To hell with it," he repeated, as he started taking a couple large strides for the sacristy located at the side of the altar. "Goodbye and good riddance," he said under his breath, several steps from the side of the altar. And then, as if a proverbial lightning bolt struck him, the pastor turned to face the congregation once more, pointing to hell, beneath their feet.

"Goodbye and good riddance, Big Media," he shouted. "Good riddance," he shouted for emphasis. Then, he strode purposefully off the altar, a smile now creasing his face.

Chapter 3:

Divided We Fall

★ ★ ★ ★ ★

"A house divided against itself cannot stand."
—Abraham Lincoln, June 16, 1858

"I sure don't feel like we're united as a country any more. In fact, we're about as far away from being united as we can get."
—Jeb, 38, Street Sweeper, Metairie, LA

"It doesn't seem like we're split into two [countries]. It seems like we're splitting into a whole bunch of different groups. Nobody gets along with anybody else anymore.'"
—Dinah, 42, Housewife, Winnetka, IL

"Listen, in this day and age, you just take care of yourself. I mean, I hate to say it. But to hell with anyone else."
—Josiah, 28, Unemployed, Sugarland, TX

After leading more than two thousand focus group sessions over the past twenty-plus years, I'd readily admit that there are few seminal moments – when time seems to stand still, a bolt of lightning might crash outside, and the immensity of what has been spoken in the focus group room hangs in the air amidst the utter silence. Sure, we remember the general outcome of each group, the characters that populate our (alternative?) universe, and even some of the brilliant (and un-brilliant) oratory that marks each group. But specific defining moments of a focus group? Those are hard to recall, even the night after a group. Especially after doing **thousands** of groups.

But on a frigid, misty night in January of 2006, in San Diego's Mission Valley, one particular comment stopped us – and our focus group – dead in our tracks. In the midst of a particularly heated discussion on illegal immigration, one small woman, Rosa, who'd been noticeably quiet up to that point, jumped up from her place at the focus group table, clearly agitated, and screamed, "I think we're headed for another Civil War. This country is falling apart!"

The room, moments before engulfed in a spirited verbal melee, suddenly fell silent. You could have heard a pin drop, even from a mile away. The moderator, trained to **always** keep the conversation moving, cleared his throat and shuffled a few papers in uncomfortable silence. The focus group respondents shifted uncomfortably in their chairs, as if considering the weight of Rosa's comment.

The focus group room remained silent, until Rosa herself broke the silence in a calm, much less agitated voice. "I don't mean to frighten anyone or try to start fights, but look around...we don't get along any more, and we are coming apart at the seams." Respondents around the table seemed to nod their heads in unison. "I wasn't born in this country," Rosa continued, "so I don't know exactly what a Civil War really is. But if it splits apart the country like I think it does, then that's where we're heading."

For the remainder of the night, the focus group discussed how the country was disintegrating before their very eyes. Almost apologetic to the moderator, the focus group respondents seemed to believe that a Civil War in the United States was somehow inevitable. It was the first time that we'd heard about the country's divisiveness in such stark, but dramatic terms during a focus group. Alas, it wouldn't be the last.

Abraham Lincoln's most famous line, noted at the start of this chapter, was uttered on the eve of the greatest crisis faced by this nation. We fought a bloody Civil War once in the United States, which threatened to derail our grand experiment with democracy and, at times, literally pitted brother against brother, neighbor against neighbor, on the battlefield. The `war was so destructive and divisive that even today, more than one hundred forty years later, we have not settled all of our differences between regions, races and political philosophies. (Recall the emotional, high-pitched battles over flying the Confederate flag in the capitols of Georgia, South Carolina and several other Southern states, just within the past few years.) The battlefield carnage was a bloody, tragic metaphor for the great divisions in our country during the 1800's; today, a rising tide of divisions which mark nearly every aspect of American life inspire a dark, foreboding question, which nobody really wants to ask but which we all **must** answer at some point…Could a Civil War happen again?

Okay, so perhaps that's an overly dramatic question – or is it? But before we can seriously address the issue, let's start with an easier, if not somewhat whimsical question. Quick now, do you live in a red state or a blue state? If you're like me, you're probably familiar with how your state tends to vote (or, more importantly, how you tend to vote). But the part that always sparks confusion is, does that make us "red" or "blue?" I never could get straight which color was linked to which party – didn't they used to be identified by the donkey and the elephant?

Of course, it's not really that important to know whether you live in a red state or a blue state – after all, the entire concept was the "brainchild" of some feeble news producer trying to punch up the meager ratings for one of the cable news networks in the wake of the divisive and controversial 2000 Presidential election. But what **is** important is the basic concept of "red" vs. "blue" – or the great divide between political parties, candidates and belief systems that plagues our country.

"Red" vs. "blue" has become a hip, pop culture reference to the best known and most widely referenced of the many emerging divisions in our country, the chasm that separates Republicans and Democrats, or Liberals and Conservatives. But as troubling as the "red" vs. "blue" division has been and continues to be, it's but the tip of the proverbial iceberg. As we approach the end of the first decade of the New Millennium, we see an America in our focus groups that is increasingly divided on a wide variety of fronts, and not just "red" vs. "blue."

The Great Divide(s)

If you aren't convinced that we live in a deeply divided society, then take a quick look around. Watch cable news or Bill Maher on HBO for a few minutes, head to a School Board or PTA meeting in your community, or even go to a local dive or watering hole. Take a drive to a bookstore and read the titles, or check the editorial pages of your local paper. If Americans have always taken pride in the concept of freedom of speech and our ability to openly disagree with each other, then this is the "proudest" of times, indeed. In fact, we aren't going to spend much, if any, time on these pages defending the proposition that we are deeply divided, because it's **so** blatantly obvious. We seem, at times, to be quite literally at each others' throats – just take a look around you.

Instead, we'll focus our efforts on the obvious issues – **how** and **why** we're divided.

With apologies to Elizabeth Barrett Browning – how are we divided? Let us count the ways, the **many different and varied** ways. Our focus groups indicate that Americans are sharply divided on everything from politics to race – and the sheer depths of our divide threaten the very fabric of our nation. Not sure you quite agree yet? Well, the comments from some of our focus group respondents are included here and are especially insightful, as they help to illustrate the tone – a nasty one, by and large – and substance of contemporary dialogue.

The Great Divide(s): How We're Divided

1. Politics
2. Education
3. Religion
4. Immigration
5. Race Relations

Politics – Thousands of years ago, Aristotle wrote, "Man is by nature a political animal." Fast forward now to the Twenty-First Century. If Aristotle meant that politics turns us all into animals, then he was truly prescient. Politics in the Twenty-First Century? As Charlie Brown might say after whiffing on a football held by the irrepressible Lucy: "ARRRRRRRRGGGGHHHHHH."

Our focus group work indicates that the vast middle of America's political spectrum – or what some commentators would call "moderates" or the "undecided" – is evaporating faster than Utah's Great Salt Lake. In fact, public opinion polls show that the number of Americans describing themselves as liberal and conservative has increased dramatically in the past three decades – essentially gutting and diminishing the traditional vast American middle.[20]

So how would we describe the tone of the political discourse in our focus groups – even the groups that have **nothing** to do with politics?

---

[20] According to Gallup's Public Opinion Survey work.

Let's try shrill, tempestuous, divisive, emotional, passionate, violent, hysterical, stormy, turbulent, partisan…

> *"I hate the other side."*
> —Marla, 24, Student, Galveston, TX

> *"Conservatives are just plain mean and deserve to die."*
> —Jon, 38, Designer, San Francisco, CA

> *"All liberals are stupid, aren't they?"*
> —Ellard, 58, CPA, Westport, CT

> *"I hope the conservatives burn in hell."*
> —T.L., 64, Retired, Urbandale, IA

> *"If you're stupid enough to vote liberal, then you deserve everything you've got coming to you."*
> —Fritz, 23, Factory Worker, Evanston, IL

These comments are just the tip of the iceberg – most aren't even taken from groups that remotely have anything to do with politics.

But the political divide is far worse than the disappearance of the middle ground and moderation. No, in our focus groups, we also see an America in which:

- There is little true/real **dialogue** between opposing sides in many of our arguments or divisions. It's as if you choose one side or the other, and once you're there, you're impervious to reason, persuasion or a maturation of your position – essentially, once you choose sides, you're a "lifer." **In essence, we've stopped listening to each other!** True, we shout at each other a lot, but the other side doesn't listen. We're merely talking over each other. And God forbid if you ever change your position…

"You've changed your mind. That's inexcusable. You should be ashamed."
—Elise, 46, Teacher, Beaverton, OR

"That guy is a flip-flopper. No way I vote for him. [He has] no guts."
—Terry, 44, Executive, Auburn, VA

- Americans have increasingly **personalized** many of our divisions – in essence, when someone disagrees with your position or your side, they seem to hate you, personally, as well as your "side."

"If you don't like the war, go hang out with your commie bastard friends."
—Juan, 52, Sanitation Worker, New York, NY

"If you're pro-abortion, don't you dare ever show up on my doorstep. You are most certainly not welcome."
—Claudia, 45, Consultant, Jupiter, FL

"I just plain don't associate with them [conservatives]. They aren't my friends."
—Billie, 19, Clerical Worker, Florissant, MO

- Many arguments are boiled down to an overly simplistic "black" vs. "white" divide, and lack a "gray" or middle-ground (dare we say it, moderate?) position. You're either one side or the other, and there's not much (if anything) in between two bitterly conflicting sides. Why, the concept of nuance is practically heresy in this increasingly divisive America. And with the loss of the proverbial middle ground, we often lose the opportunity for a compromise – or a solution.

"Let them liberals stay on their side. I don't want to have anything to do with them."
—Lisa, 38, Unemployed, Palo Alto, CA

"I really don't give a damn why you feel the way you do. That's your problem."
—Elsa, 46, Personnel, Encino, CA

"Don't tell me about your side. I am not interested, at all. You got it?"
—Willie T., 42, Insurance, Poughkeepsie, NY

<u>Education</u> – This isn't even a battle between one side versus another, but, rather, a total free-for-all. Virtually **nobody** is happy with our American education system. Our focus groups indicate that the majority of Americans believe that our public school system is turning out lazy, simple-minded Americans with an aptitude for little more than flipping burgers. And the discord isn't solely focused on the quality of our education system. We are deeply divided on charter schools and private schools, compensation for teachers, lack of discipline in our schools, safety for children (in the wake of Columbine and Virginia Tech), the influence of unions in schools and a host of other issues.

"Teachers are just plain lazy. Damn lazy."
—Ida, 51, Secretary, Golden, CO

"I don't respect my son's teachers. At all. That's why I hate the parent-teacher day. It makes my skin crawl."
—Ishbien, 40, Office Worker, Staten Island, NY

"It's gotten to the point where I feel bad when my kids head off to school every day. I almost want to cry."
—Jim, 33, Executive, Morristown, NJ

"I worry so much about my kids in school. It's awful, really. It's sure not the same America I grew up in."
—Benton, 40, City Worker, Rosedale, MN

<u>Religion</u> – We are, according to many Americans, in the midst of a Holy War, a war of good vs. evil. That's the obvious religious strife – America vs. the Islamic jihadists or fascists who are determined to

overthrow our way of life and such prized values as religious tolerance. This battle rages daily all over the world (i.e., in Iraq and Afghanistan), including here in the U.S. And if you think it's not raging here in the U.S., read the chilling quotes below from two of our focus group respondents:

"I don't pray for America to be destroyed, but if it's Allah's will, so be it. It would not bother me, either. Praise be Allah."
—Mohammed, 41, City Worker, San Jose, CA

"As long as America pursues this lifestyle, it will be destroyed. Whether by the hand of God or the hand of man, it will be destroyed."
—Braeden, 59, Retired, Bellevue, WA

Less obvious is the war against religion by the group Bill O'Reilly sometimes dubs as "secular progressives." They're not religious and don't really want **any** Americans to be very devoted to religion or faith. The secularists often defend their attacks on religion under the guise of separation of church and state, but when we talk to them in depth, it's clear that the real goal is a separation of God and the everyday lives of Americans – they want God removed from our society, day-to-day, permanently. (These are the people who want religion removed from Christmas displays.)

"If you want to do stuff with your God, do it behind closed doors. But keep it away from me, from everybody. Don't make it a part of our society and push it off on me. Keep it to yourself."
—Rachel, 50, Teacher, Lexington, KY

Immigration – One of the easiest lessons to learn at Focus Group Moderator Training School is also one of the shortest. If you are ever involved in a focus group that is exceedingly dull and quiet, and want to stir up the crowd to participate, there is but one magic word to utter: **"immigration."**

Indeed, this one simple word, "immigration," can stir up long, passionate, multi-faceted arguments and debates – and literally has done so across this great country over the past decade as millions of illegal immigrants have crossed into our United States and changed the way we live. Are they supporting our economy by doing jobs no one wants to do? Or are they taking livelihoods away from native-born citizens? Are they a drain on social programs, or do they contribute heavily into our dwindling Social Security system? Do they represent a security threat, or…the arguments over immigration seem to carry on forever, certainly with more time and complexity than we can devote here.

Recent polling by Gallup shows that, while Americans still continue to support the concept of immigration in the abstract, support for increasing or enhancing immigration – from support for increasing the number of immigrants to supporting President George W. Bush's policies on immigration – has waned in recent months.

Regardless of how you, personally, net out on the issue of immigration, we know that the immigration debate is fiery, indeed, at least in our focus groups.

"We ought to arrest every damn one of them [the illegal immigrants]."
—Phillip, 44, Executive, Dulles, VA

"I mean, we've all been immigrants at one time. That is so hypocritical to pretend like we're not."
—Sheila, 49, Executive, Aurora, IL

"If they find an employer who hires illegals, they ought to be put out of business that day. No questions asked. It should just be automatic."
—Bill, 40, High School Administrator, Omaha, NE

"These people pay taxes, they are the hard workers in our society. Without them, our economy wouldn't survive. They are just God-fearing people trying to raise their families honestly."
—Phil, 37, Teacher, Irvine, CA

"That's crap. They are over here to make money and send it back to Mexico. They take jobs from working class Americans. And they cost us plenty. They go to our colleges and public schools. Why can't they come over here legally, like all of our relatives did? Because they're cheating, that's why. I say send 'em to jail. Now who's with me on that?"
—Izell, 33, Unemployed, West Covina, CA

How else are we divided? Well, the news only gets worse…

Race Relations – A myriad of statistical and anecdotal sources indicate continued improvement in racial equality in the United States. For instance, per capita income for African-Americans has soared in the past thirty-five years, from just under $2,000 per person to more than $16,000 in 2005 – a whopping increase of more than 800%. Better still, the gap in income between White Americans and Black Americans has narrowed considerably.[21]

Alas, while race relations have improved, our focus groups indicate that we are still a long way away from true equality, when the color of our skin, or our racial heritage, matter little.

Throughout this book, I've pledged to provide a plethora of unedited comments to help illustrate what people are saying in the thousands of focus groups that we've moderated. However, this one section is the exception. To provide the plethora of racially charged statements – unedited – would only seem to fan the flames of racial strife. So, with apologies, I am providing only a very narrow/limited set

---

[21] Taken from the 2006 New York Times Almanac.

of supporting statements from our focus groups in the area of race relations or racial equality.

> *"Black people are still a major pain in the ass."*
> —Bill, 40 (No details on who he is, for security purposes.)

> *"White people still act like they are God's gift."*
> —Shirell, 38 (No details on who she is, for security purposes.)

> *"I try to be nice to all the colored people in my life. That's what we're supposed to do, I guess. Isn't that right?"*
> —Abe, 71 (No details on who he is, for security purposes.)

Think for a moment about Democratic Senator (and presidential candidate) Barack Obama's pastor, the infamous Jeremiah Wright. During the campaign for the White House in 2008, the good Reverend sparked a fierce nationwide debate with incendiary remarks from past pulpit speeches which included comparing the U.S. (unfavorably) to Al Qaeda, claims that the government introduced AIDS to kill African Americans, and claims that the 9/11 terrorist attacks were "earned" or warranted based, in part, on our many sins against Black South Africans. The race war over with? On that front, Reverend Wright probably wanted to paraphrase one of Al Pacino's most famous screen lines, from *Scent of a Woman*, "We're just getting started!"

If the most famous – or infamous — source of racial in-fighting in this country remains the traditional "black versus white" battle, make no mistake that other racial divides have emerged. In our focus groups, it is evident that **many** Americans are still racist toward other Americans with a different skin color of any sort, or any type of non-traditional ethnic background. Specifically, our focus groups indicate several other ethnic origins that are emerging as targets of widespread, and "heartfelt" racial bias:

Hispanics – Technically speaking, it's Mexicans who comprise the majority of immigrants – legal and illegal – to the U.S. at this point. But not in the minds of dimwitted racists. No, they see anyone of Hispanic descent as fostering our problem with illegal immigration. Consequently, they tend to hate Hispanics, on the basis of their skin color and heritage.

> *"I am so tired of Spics swimming across the Rio Grande and creating problems in this country. I hate them"*
> —Reid, 50, Insurance, Littleton, CO

- **Arabs/Muslims** – Like Hispanics, Arabs and Muslims are "guilty" in the minds of most Americans, simply because of the dastardly deeds of a handful of terrorists. Based on the rhetoric in focus groups, we expect the problems with this form of racial and religious intolerance to grow markedly in coming years.

  > *"I think these Muslims are the devil himself."*
  > —Alma, 48, Peachtree, GA

  > *"We should kill ten Arabs for every American they kill in a terrorist attack."*
  > —Bill, 38 (No details on who he is, for security purposes.)

- **Indians** – We don't mean American Indians, who've long faced their own forms of discrimination in this country; no, the current trend is racial bigotry against continental Indians from the Far East. And their primary sin in this matter? Not idolatry of cows, war with Bangladesh, or devotion to Gandhi. No, they're simply guilty, in the minds of bigots, of taking customer service and high-tech jobs that could be filled by "real" Americans.

"The Indians act peaceful and all, but they're really waging economic war against us. And they're winning, too."
—Anette, 39, Child Care, San Ysidro, CA

- **Asians** – We continually hear harsh criticism of Asian-Americans in focus groups. But the root of this criticism often appears to be little more than petty envy of the economic success of Asians. In other words, many Americans aren't sure why they dislike them so much – but are sure that they do.

"Every convenience store that you run into is owned by a Chinaman. I swear."
—Sal, 58, City Worker, New Rochelle, NY

"It's true that the Asians keep to themselves. But they are out there buying up our country while our back is turned."
—Bob, 44, Carpenter, Fullerton, CA

"I just plain don't trust anyone with slanty eyes."
—A.C., 62, Retired, Los Angeles, CA

<u>Privacy</u> – One of my favorite movie lines was uttered by Daniel Stern in *City Slickers*. Stern, a rather unassuming sort in the film who runs a grocery store for his father-in-law, finally loses his temper at his (soon to be ex-) wife, and roars, unapologetically, "If hate were people, then I'd be China." Well, if **privacy** was a person/people, it would be diagnosed as schizophrenic.

Indeed, we can't seem to make up our minds on this pesky privacy issue, and are increasingly at odds with each other. On the one hand, some of us desperately want to avoid another bloody terrorist attack such as 9/11, and are willing to give up some privacy and civil liberties to protect the homeland. This group of Americans generally supports wire taps of suspected terrorists, harsh methods of interrogation of suspected terrorists, and even such banal terror prevention methods as monitoring of withdrawals of books from local libraries.

> *"I don't give a damn if my neighbors know that I reserved 'Gone With The Wind' from the library, especially if doing that kind of thing prevents an attack. What have I got to hide?"*
> —Bill, 42, Retail, West Hartford, CT

"What have I got to hide?" really sums up the group of Americans that isn't so much anti-privacy as much as they simply don't consider privacy a priority. In this era of computers, the Internet, wireless phone and the like, these Americans generally feel as if their life is an open book, from American Express knowing what they buy with credit cards to database marketing firms estimating their wealth. The bottom line is that they're less concerned with closing the book than closing the door on terrorism.

In contrast, many other Americans value privacy seemingly above all else, and are unwilling to forego **any** privacy for the promise of enhanced security. And that's part of the issue for this group of civil libertarians – they are highly skeptical and doubt whether lost privacy really enhances the security of the homeland. For instance, are law enforcement officials listening to the amorous conversations of a teenaged couple in the Midwest more likely to stop terrorism or to get off on their prurient interest in the conversations of the lovelorn and restless?

> *"I don't want anyone to know anything about me. Ever. Period."*
> —Hal, 44, Semi-Retired, Austin, TX

But beyond this group's skepticism, we've noticed that they just plain believe that privacy is an American birthright – like equality. During our focus groups, many of these respondents even cite (mistakenly, I believe) Constitutional guarantees regarding privacy.

> *"Don't one of them Amendments say that people can't know*
> *nothing about you? I'm sure that it does."*
> —Billie, 58, Disability Instructor, Hialeah, FL

What makes this issue even more tangled is that many Americans are on both sides of the issue. Now, without making you feel bad, take a good look in the mirror after this paragraph. Are you concerned about the erosion of privacy? But do you also have a personal page or web site on a social interaction site such as Facebook, My Space, or Bebo, presumably to inform the world about everything from your favorite song and color to your philosophy on life? Keep in mind that virtually anybody can access this material. We thought so. Millions of us Americans do. This is the nature of our schizophrenia on this issue.

Think we're exaggerating? Think again. Recall the strange case of Ashley Alexandra Dupre, aka Kristen, the call-girl who blew up New York Governor Eliot Spitzer's (aka, No.9?) career in March of 2008. Days after the Governor's resignation, numerous pictures of Dupre appeared online and in the media, including several pictures of Dupre in a bikini obtained by the Associated Press from her MySpace page. In other words, Dupre herself had published the photos for all the world to see on her site. Yet, within days, her attorney, Don D. Buchwald, complained about the publication of photos and vowed to protect his client's interests. What better example could there be of our schizophrenia, or of battling ourselves over the privacy issue? A prostitute promotes her life on MySpace, yet complains (through her attorney) when images from these very pages are used by the news media in the wake of her participation in one of the decade's biggest sex scandals. Schizophrenic, indeed.

In truth, we could continue this discussion regarding our divisions for pages and pages – indeed, for the rest of the book. But we have so much more we need to discuss in these limited pages. So at the risk of skipping over compelling material, we're simply going to list some of the other divisions which plague our great country. Keep in mind that this list is far from complete, and is not presented in any particular order.

Divisions in the U.S., Circa 2008

- **Homosexual Rights/Gay Marriage**
- **The Iraq War**
- **Gang Wars**
- **Age Conflicts**
- **The Battle Over Christmas**
- **Obama Vs. McCain**
- **Religious Zealots vs. Agnostics/ Secularists**
- **English-First vs. Those Who Prefer Other Languages**

- **Criminal Rights vs. Victim Rights**
- **Pro-Life vs. Pro-Choice**
- **Growing Road Rage**
- **Lawsuit Abuse**
- **Global Warming**
- **Gender Abuse**
- **Domestic Partnership vs. Marriage**
- **Class Warfare – i.e., the Middle Class vs. The Upper Class**

That we're divided is an inescapable conclusion for readers of this book, in my view. But what's more critical than the nature of our divisions is the root causes for these dangerous fissures – why has this country begun literally splitting apart over the past decade? As it turns out, I am very grateful to have spent more than twenty years moderating focus groups – as focus groups provide unique and compelling insight into this most vexing problem. Why are we divided? Focus groups provide an understanding and insight that we've not been able to discern from other sources, to date.

I'm often asked how, or if, focus groups have changed over time – now that I'm an "old timer" who's spent a good portion of his life involved in this pursuit. Coincidentally, the biggest change in focus groups over the past two decades also happens to be one of the primary drivers of the divisiveness which now plagues our country. Over time, we've come to call it the **"Cable News Effect."**

The "Cable News Effect" is an approach to debate and discussion which accentuates differences, and does little, if anything, to promote a common understanding or to solve problems. TV news has virtually assured that this is the one and only way that we deal with differences – as a TV debate.

Once upon a time, TV news consisted largely of taped reports introduced by an anchor. This format thrust Walter Cronkite and a host of other journalists to exalted positions in our country, as the major networks communicated the news of the day. But the advent of satellite uplinks in the 1980's allowed news programs to interject a "live" element into broadcasts – i.e., the infamous "talking head" element of news. This technology eventually drove the advent of shows like "Crossfire" on CNN in which two competing sides of every issue were argued about for most of a half hour. (Notice that we said that these problems were argued about; not that problems were solved or differences narrowed.)

Eventually, shows such as ABC's Nightline and CNN's Crossfire allowed guests to debate each other – and what should have been a quantum leap forward in debating the news actually sparked the "Cable News Effect." So what, exactly, is the "Cable News Effect?"

The "Cable News Effect" refers, quite literally, to the impact of the way we cover TV news and the way in which we debate, discuss and solve (or don't solve) issues in this country.

"You know the way CNN does it. They have both sides of every issue. And you argue your side of the issue on the air and hope that people think you've won when all the arguing is done. I'd guess you'd call that the CNN Effect, or something like that, right?"
—Aldus, 69, Retired, St. Paul, MN

Guests hash, re-hash, argue and even snipe at each other during cable news shows, but solve and/or agree upon very little. The "Cable News Effect" accentuates our differences – mightily at times (isn't that the entertainment value of TV news?) – but does very little (or nothing) to promote common understanding or agreement. The "Cable News Effect" guarantees that we promote, ferment and celebrate differences, but almost never find common ground on **any** type of problem or issue. Throughout the thousands of focus groups we've conducted over the past twenty years, we've even noticed a set of "rules of engagement" for the "Cable news Effect" – a rather troubling pattern to the way in which Americans discuss debate and don't solve or smooth over our differences.

Rules Of Engagement:

The Cable News Effect

1) **Every issue has two – and only two – sides, which are typically diametrically opposed.** There is no room for subtlety or shades of grey when it comes to such differences. On every issue, there is a black, and a white – nothing more, nothing less.

2) **There is no middle ground on any issue or subject – only different, opposing sides.**

3) **Make the case for your side of the issue – and never consider the merits of the other side.** Tune that out, if at all possible. (That's why TV guests often "talk over" each other.)

4) **Most issues can be boiled down to very simplistic sound bites.** Never concede the complexities of an issue – always strive to simplify!

5) **Never shown any empathy or understanding for the opposing view of an issue, for that is a sure sign of weakness.** Remember, your side is **always** morally right, and the other side is just plain wrong.

6) **Issues do not evolve or change over time. So there can certainly be no evolution or maturity in your thinking on a given issue.** What you think today is simply the way it is – and it will not change.

If you're not sure what to make of our assertion that there's a "Cable News Effect" at work in this country, then I challenge you to spend an hour or two, if not a day or two, watching television news. You're challenged to point out a single instance where the TV debate has narrowed differences or solved a problem – to the best of my knowledge, **it has never, ever happened.** It's far more likely that a TV news debate will exacerbate and deepen a divide. (We formally challenge every reader of this book to satisfy our challenge – we would love to be proven wrong.)

A greater concern is that the "Cable News Effect" is no longer a TV phenomenon; it's been exported to every aspect of American life, as we've noted in our focus groups. This is how we deal with debate, controversy, and disagreement in the United States – and it's not a positive change. Try to get a group of your friends together, and spark some sort of issue or debate. Try it at work. See how many "Rules Of Engagement" from our list earlier in this chapter ring true.

Of greater importance, when is that last time we debated and solved a critical issue in this country? Again, I challenge you, dear readers, to point this out to me.

As we've taken great pains to point out, this country has not been more divided since the Civil War, and it's clear that the "Cable News Effect" has contributed in a major way to this (potentially) tragic outcome. But it's far from the only major contributing factor to our country's disunity.

Another fundamental change in focus groups has also contributed to our country's disunity. During the course of the many focus groups we've led over the past two decades, we've noted the rising impact of **political correctness** on our inability to solve any problems or find common understanding on any issue.

Political correctness generally refers to language, ideas, policies, or behavior seen as seeking to minimize offense to racial, cultural, or other identity groups. In other words, political correctness is the enemy of good focus groups. When respondents discuss issues or concepts in politically correct terms, they reek of insincerity. At its most basic, political correctness is saying what you **don't** believe – no matter how exalted or desirable the goal of the deception. Through the years, some of the most common politically correct statements – which are later proven untrue in the very same focus groups in which the comments were originally uttered – include:

Typical POV's Of PC FG Respondents

- Acceptance/tolerance of homosexuality.

- Acceptance/tolerance of one or both major political parties in the U.S.

- Racial tolerance.

- Claiming to be far more affluent than we really are.

- Religious tolerance.

- Sexual tolerance, especially in areas relating to inappropriate sexual advances and behaviors related to sexual harassment.

And therein lays the problem. We won't be able to solve problems, bridge gaps or find common ground when we continually misstate our beliefs. We believe that adherence to the doctrine of political correctness forestalls any serious action to find common ground on many issues – not just those listed above. It allows Americans to feel comfortable about talking the talk, but never walking the walk. We say one thing, and mean quite another. And as long as political correctness remains so prevalent, we are unlikely to confront our major problems, much less solve them.

One specific aspect of political correctness that's caused serious rifts in this country is the concept of **"tolerance."** In our focus groups, it's clear that many Americans confuse tolerance with deception. In other words, many of us claim to embrace the concept of tolerance, while admitting in focus groups that we are anything **but** tolerant.

> *"I know that we were taught to like gays in school, but honestly, I hate them. I don't want anything to do with them."*
> —Rael, 51, Teacher, Alton, IL

> *"I admit I pretend to like them [African-Americans] to show that I'm tolerant. But honestly, I don't like them."*
> —Billie, 41, Clerical, Boston, MA

Another major contributing factor to our country's disunity, based on this focus group work, is **immigration**. No, not the concept of immigration itself – after all, many of the builders of this great country were immigrants – but the **type of immigration** we're experiencing at the dawn of the 21st Century.

Late in the Nineteenth and early in the Twentieth centuries, the majority of immigrants to the United States were of European descent. Based on interviews with some of these immigrants and their descendants, it is clear that a major initial goal of the immigrants was assimilation – they wanted to be an American first, and were only too happy to shed the vestiges of their previous lives. They weren't necessarily embarrassed about who they were or where they came from, but they were very determined to become what they perceived to be an "American."

We've spent many hours talking with recent or current immigrants in focus group rooms, and it's very clear that **things have changed** dramatically. Today's immigrants are not, on balance, keenly interested in assimilation – in many cases, it's the furthest thing from their minds – or becoming an American. Instead, they view the United States as a resource, or economic way station, on their journey through life. The U.S. is an economic life preserver which these immigrants are only too happy to grasp. But many care little about putting down permanent roots in this country.

This has become problematic over time, as the "new" immigrant population has soared into the tens of millions. The "new" immigrants, as you'll recall, are not terribly interested in assimilating into our population or becoming true Americans. Consequently, they often do not share our values and beliefs on many key issues. For instance, during focus groups, it's often clear that these immigrants are not familiar with our Constitution or Bill of Rights, our national holidays, or even great historical figures like George Washington. So how can we expect them to reach a consensus with us on anything from whether we should sanction Yuletide displays to whether we should have gone to war in Iraq?

Perhaps the most startling example of the disunity wrought by the "new" immigration was a focus group conducted with a group of young Hispanic males just before the start of the Iraq War. Out of ten males in the room, not a single one supported the U.S. attacking terrorist camps in Afghanistan, much less the U.S. making a unilateral move into Iraq. Now, reasonable people had varying opinions on this war, so that, in and of itself, is not so terribly shocking.

What was shocking was how the discussion evolved when our client had us ask these males what they would do if the U.S. attacked Mexico, with cause. (I don't recall the specific circumstance, but it was some sort of hypothetical involving Mexico stealing nuclear secrets from the U.S.). Nine out of the ten males in the room indicated that, despite working in the U.S. for a minimum of four years, and up to twenty years for one individual, they would absolutely enlist in the Mexican Army and take up arms against the U.S. When the discussion turned to whether they would attack a former friend in the U.S. as part of this war, not a single person expressed any reluctance to do so. Americans, they all agreed, would have to pay for their government's actions – and they themselves were certainly not Americans. They just worked here.

The bottom line is that we are increasingly "balkanized" – as more people living here refuse to become Americans and share our culture, values, and beliefs, it will become increasingly difficult to find common ground.

It is also increasingly clear that **technology** is contributing to greater isolation and difficulty in finding common ground in this country. We've become increasingly isolated from each other through technology tools such as cell phones, PDA's, and PC's with Internet access, to name but a few. As a consequence, we spend less time communicating directly with each other, and spend even less time **with** each other (that is, in each other's company). So is it any wonder that we are increasingly isolated and at odds with each other? (In fairness, this technology poses a problem for the whole world, not just the United States.)

One other factor that has contributed to the growing disunity in the United States is our **penchant for privacy** and **isolation**. Increasingly in focus groups, we encounter respondents who are quite withdrawn from society; they don't see themselves as members of a neighborhood, community or a city; rather, they view themselves as citizens of Planet Earth. These individuals have largely withdrawn from their local communities or cities, and mostly want to be left alone. Typically, they are social misfits who participate little in community or civic activities. In many cases, they aren't even proud to be American – they simply live here.

> *"I'm not really a citizen of anywhere. I just live here, if you know what I mean."*
> —Sally, 44, Administrative Assistant, Chantilly, VA

Still United States?

I still remember the scene… and shudder.

In one of the last episodes of Carl Sagan's landmark sci-fi series, **Cosmos,** the great astronomer was perched in a spaceship floating softly, keeping a silent vigil over his beloved planet Earth from a nearby orbit. However, as the scene unfolds, Sagan's beautiful view of Earth is sadly interrupted by brilliant flashes of light, explosions, and, ultimately, the implosion of the planet itself. Near tears, the intrepid astronomer Sagan explained that, in a moment of madness, someone on Earth had launched a nuclear conflagration which, ultimately, destroyed the planet. I can almost feel Sagan's profound sadness over this dramatic turn, even today. All I could wonder then, and now, is why, oh why would anyone do this to our beloved Earth?

Fortunately, Sagan's dramatic turn hasn't been borne out, as Earth remains spinning on its axis, soaring madly through the vastness of space. But the horror etched on Sagan's face as he watches his beloved Earth explode is very much akin to the way we feel about the United States today – are we drawing closer to the tragic end of our beloved country?

While the immigration issue remains "up in the air" politically – there's no telling what may happen – many of the other factors cited earlier in this chapter as contributing to the disunity in this country are, in our view, likely to continue unabated for at least several more years, if not longer. If we, like Sagan, were floating above looking down on our country, this fact alone might cause us to tear up – the challenges to our great Union roll merrily on, with little cause for hope.

So if we were floating above looking down on our future, what would we see with respect to disunity?

For starters, we expect a period in the next decade of social and political upheaval, similar to 1960's radicalism. No, it won't be exactly the same, but we're likely to see and experience a lot of the same elements as in the 1960's.

Future Radicalism/Protest?

Violent protests.

Political violence and/or assassination.

Attacks – i.e., bombings and the like - on some of the foundations and institutions of our country.

The development of new political movements and parties.

Increased violence against prominent private citizens.

However, we think the coming period of upheaval may make the 1960's look quaint, by comparison. Our ability to kill and mutilate far exceeds what we knew in the 1960's – apparently it's even possible to build a nuclear device in a suitcase/briefcase, and not just in the movies. All that we're lacking at the moment is the will to use such doomsday devices. But if you'd conducted as many focus group sessions as I have, you'd know that Americans are really seething beneath the surface. Not all will explode, but some seem likely to. After all, haven't we witnessed moments of domestic terrorism over the past decade or so – environmentalists burning down houses, mass murders on campus, and a sociopath like Timothy McVeigh blowing up a federal building?

We also expect, in the short-term, to see an increase in **religious and racial intolerance and persecution.** Hate crimes, lynchings, and more subtle forms of racial and religious persecution are all possible. This "melting pot" seems far more like a Vegas buffet at the moment – the food isn't melted together into one delicious treat, so much as presented together, yet every item is still separate and isolated on the buffest cart. Again, we see dissatisfaction with the many factions in our society bubbling beneath the surface. We believe that we are at the dawn of a racial and religious powder keg, one with a very short fuse.

Finally, we expect America's international position to weaken further in the near future. Once, we were envied by much of the world for our democratic form of government and economic supremacy. But the less united Americans appear to the outside world, the less likely we are to exert any real world leadership. Who we Americans are, and what we stand for, has never been more confusing in many corners of the globe. Thus, we lead by force or by habit, rather than because we exert any real moral or ethical leadership in the world

Would Carl Sagan shed tears if his futuristic spaceship floated above the United States today? Based on the focus groups I've watched and listened to over the past twenty years, it's likely that Sagan would sob, like a baby.

Chapter 4:

Take This Job And...

MBC & The Radical

Transformation Of The

American Workplace

✯ ✯ ✯ ✯ ✯

"Work sure has changed since I got out of college. The people, the hours, even what we work on, sure is different."
—John, 42, Executive, Englewood, CO

The auditorium was so empty that you could literally hear a pin drop. But just seconds later, a loud bell tore through the silence, noisily announcing the hordes about to descend into the auditorium. Then, the doors on each side of the small stage blasted open, and a relentless stream of students headed up the steps, filling the back and, eventually, most of the front seats, too.

*The students were having a grand old time, sharing stories of weekend partying, the Green Day concert from the past week, and other lighthearted moments of college life. Then, just when it seemed that that they were having **too** much fun, a tall, bald professor, his fringe hair rolled into tiny gray curls, entered and slammed his text down onto the stage lectern. As if trained, the students immediately fell silent, and the professor began lecturing in a loud monotone, conditioned by years in this and other auditoriums.*

After a few minutes of administrative fluff, he appeared to get down to business. "Alright class, let's turn to today's material. Who wants to tell me what "Management By Chaos" is? Alright, let's start with...

Management By Chaos (MBC)

Unfortunately, I can't bring you the full lecture on "Management By Chaos" in these pages, mainly because it's never occurred! To the best of our knowledge, MBC is a concept that we've developed at my company, Marketing Advocates, Inc., based on analyzing thousands of focus groups over the past twenty years. (A Google search on the subject turned up plenty of citations for "Chaos Management" but little or nothing under our term, "Management By Chaos.")

But that begs the question – why would we want to bring you this lecture in the first place? Because, quite simply, Management By Chaos is one of the biggest changes in the American workplace that we've observed over the past decade or so. MBC and several other changes are literally transforming the American workplace as we enter this new century.

First, a bit of background for you readers. Not all of our focus groups have been consumer groups, with every day, average Americans. No, we've done literally hundreds of focus groups with business people from a wide variety of industries, in which we've discussed everything from how they work to how they play (after work). And from these focus groups, the concept of MBC was born.

It's our view that the advent of MBC – or Management By Chaos – is the **single most critical change** in the way that we Americans work and conduct business over the past ten to twenty years. It is a philosophy, an organizing principle, and even a way of life for most American managers. As we describe MBC in depth, perhaps you can relate it to how you and your friends, colleagues and co-workers manage and work in the current American economy.

"What you're saying may be right. And that problem could be super-critical in the future. But it's not my job to worry about problems out in the future. It's my job to manage our problems today, okay?"
—Petia, 44, Office Manager, Los Angeles, CA

"We have a saying at our company. Don't worry today about tomorrow's problems."
—Parson, 56, Company President, Apple Valley, MN

The famed astronomer Carl Sagan once noted that, in order to truly bake an apple pie from scratch, one must first invent the universe. (Think about it; the logic is unassailable!) Well, **MBC is a concept which implies that in order for Americans to manage and make decisions in business, they must <u>first</u> be faced with, or must be experiencing, chaos, or crisis.** Now, chaos in business can take many forms – lack of resources (say, money), lack of staff, severe time pressures, or significant competition, to name but a few examples. Regardless, what we've observed is that until and unless the moment when confronted with chaos or a major problem, American managers don't (manage, that is).

In lay terms, MBC is a term or philosophy which reflects the contemporary penchant for managing by the seat-of-the-pants, focusing solely on the short-term (the here-and-now) at the expense of long-term decisions. We don't seem to want to take action in business **until** faced with a problem, crisis or chaos which is impacting us **today**. It's somewhat like a basketball game – the game may be forty-eight minutes long, but the action doesn't really start until the last two minutes.

As has been mentioned, a significant part of the MBC philosophy is its focus on **today**. In other words, MBC is relatively unconcerned with what **might** happen down the road, no matter how dangerous or problematic the future may be; it's far more concerned with today's problems.

"I just can't spend time worrying about what's going to happen down the road. I've just got too much on my plate today."
—Claudia, 51, Chief Executive, Pittsburgh, PA

Perhaps the concept is best illustrated with a few examples – actual reasons why businesses hired us to do focus groups just in the last few years:

- A company introduces a new product to the market, despite their own internal research which shows the product is somewhat (or maybe even seriously) flawed. Only when sales lag about six months later – and the company is clearly being hurt in the pocketbook – do they finally authorize focus groups to figure out specifically why consumers aren't buying the product.

- A company which for years has marketed toys as prizes or rewards in arcade games is suddenly fired by its largest distributor. Only at this point do they decide to do focus groups to figure out what mix of toys would be most popular with its target audience, to ensure that they don't get fired by any more of their distributors. (Talk about closing the barn door after the animals have fled!) Of course, had they done the research before being fired, they might be sitting pretty today, with their largest distribution agreement in tact.

- A major restaurant chain has been marketing its food for nearly a decade. Only after their largest competitor has a record year do they decide to conduct focus groups to ascertain their competitive position and identify their weaknesses, relative to this major competitor.

- A telecom company had invested – and no, this isn't a typo – **billions** of dollars in its network and in major acquisitions. However, only after more than twenty consecutive quarters of losses and lack of growth, when stockholders lambasted management and demanded change, did they decide to conduct focus groups on how customers viewed their products. Up until then, they had been "flying blind," as we like to say in the focus group business.

In each case, management clearly managed **only** for the here-and-now, not the near or distant future, certainly – and were compelled to act only when faced with a major problem or crisis. Yet, in each case, management easily could have conducted focus groups months, years, or decades in advance to ward off the emerging problem **before it ever became a problem**. But that's not how MBC works – in a nutshell, it's all about today.

In fairness, businesses failing to act until first confronted by a crisis, or chaos, isn't restricted to our focus group clients, or the need to conduct focus groups. Take, for instance, the housing industry. In the early 2000's, the industry was the most profitable it had ever been. From California to Colorado to Florida, housing manufacturers were raking in record profits as Americans benefited from low interest rates and a booming economy.

But by early 2008, the bubble had burst, spectacularly so. You probably know the story – sub-prime lending at the same time as $100 a barrel oil was a combustible mix which led to a recession for the country, and a depression for the housing industry. But had the housing industry prepared for this steep downturn? Had the industry reinvested record profits in something other than a CEO's fat golden parachute? Did they develop new products and services to meet the needs of more austere consumers during a downturn? Did they limit their investments in new developments, land and other speculative ventures while cash-strapped consumers stopped buying? Why, you know the answer to all of these questions, don't you?

"We just manage quarter by quarter here."
—Caleb, 29, Marketing Assistant for Home Builder, Denver, CO

The reality is that the housing industry is one of the chief practitioners of MBC, waiting until the sub-prime lending industry became a full-fledged fiasco before finally reacting to the situation. Housing executives rode the "ups" and "downs" of our cyclical American economy much like a surfer on Waikiki Beach, spending precious little time, if any, planning for the future. They just never figured that they were riding a monster, rogue wave on the way down.

If it's not readily apparent, you should know that MBC hasn't been much of a positive for the American economy, in our view. While it can be argued that MBC has forced American managers, in some cases, to take decisive action and respond quickly, if not forcefully, to changing business conditions, its impact, overall, appears to be largely negative. Specifically, our extensive focus groups and in-depth interviews with business practitioners indicate that the primary problems with MBC have included:

A short-term orientation/focus – MBC is all about waiting until there **is** a problem in the here and now before taking action, any action. Literally, American managers don't look to the future – see how management of American companies has responded to spiking oil prices in 2008, the emerging national economic recession, the housing depression, or other recent problems to affirm this tendency.

You've heard the frequent complaint about stockholders or a corporate board focusing on the short-term/near-term? It's our contention that this mostly reflects the plethora of MBC managers in our contemporary economy. They don't manage to enhance long-term shareholder value. They manage via MBC – for today.

"We really don't take strong action until the market warrants it."
—Suzie, 49, Executive, Peoria, IL

MBC is reactive, not proactive – Managers only react to emerging problems or chaos; they are **not** motivated to take action against, or forestall, **potential** problems. Take, for instance, management response to rising fuel costs in the domestic airline industry. Once upon a time – i.e., a few short years ago – oil was $40, $50, or even $70 a barrel. During "good" times like these, is it not possible that a few major airlines might have taken action of some sort to reduce the strain should oil head above $100 a barrel? Perhaps they could have negotiated more price certainty, established some sort of collective organization to purchase fuel to reduce costs, or even worked with the federal government to tap our country's Strategic Petroleum Reserve when prices spiked. Not a chance, at least in a world dominated by Management By Chaos. Only when oil topped $115 a barrel did the airline industry cut capacity and increase fuel surcharges on air fares. Of course, by then, it was too late to truly impact profitability. Let the red ink flow!

> *"We see problems, and then we go and fix them."*
> —Paul, 39, General Manager, White Plains, NY

Inefficiency – Ultimately, MBC is nothing if not inefficient as a business strategy. MBC managers don't usually take action until it's far too late, when they have few viable alternatives to combat the emerging chaos. In our view, it's somewhat like managing personal health – you can try preventative care to make sure that you're never seriously ill, or you can react to serious health problems only after they emerge – often with a limited set of prescriptive health remedies. Hence, in the last decade, MBC has yielded melt-downs at major American companies like Enron, Qwest, Level 3, AOL and MCI, as well as the S & L mess, the "dot-com bust," the housing downturn and other financial scandals. All in all, MBC has basically left behind a legacy of crisis.

> *"Sometimes, there isn't much we can do by the time we try to fix a problem. Our hands are tied."*
> —Carla, 49, Executive, Coral Gables, FL

The Impact Of MBC

Clearly, the economy has grown, and rather substantially, over the past twenty years. So how could the MBC philosophy have negatively impacted our economy, if we're growing so quickly? (Okay, so some of you readers may go so far as to think I'm crazy and don't know what I'm talking about!)

It's true that the American economy has grown, and steadily, over the past twenty years. But I would contend that MBC has been a major drain on this growth, in much the same way that a fifty mile an hour headwind slows down a cross-country jetliner. Sure, the airliner still speeds across the sky, but its speed is diminished significantly by the drag on the wings.

So if our economy has continued to grow steadily **despite** the rise of Management By Chaos, it's natural to wonder why MBC has emerged despite its negative economic impact.

The short answer is that MBC is driven by several factors which are beyond society's control, and which may be operating to drive MBC in a stealth-like fashion – i.e., behind-the-scenes. In the course of conducting thousands of focus groups, we've definitely observed some of the key factors which underlie MBC:

FACTORS WHICH DRIVE MBC

➢ *Technology*

➢ *Poor Training*

➢ *Instant Gratification*

➢ *Laziness*

Technology – Without question, technology has sped up the pace at which we conduct business, providing the "infrastructure" for the emergence of MBC. Cell phones, FAX machines, pagers and the like have allowed Americans to sit back and wait until a crisis emerges before acting, because we can seemingly respond to emerging conditions **instantaneously**. For this reason, we've developed tools like "Just In Time" inventory management, which allows manufacturers to produce goods and ship them only when needed. We also have touchpads at Hertz which manage their inventory of rental cars on a real-time basis.

"We don't panic. We wait until real problems emerge."
—Sam, 36, Manager, Mesa, AZ

"Technology is great. It's allowed us to do a much better job of managing our inventory."
—Harold, 54, Manager, Florissant, MO

On their face, these technology tools are actually very positive for the American economy and undoubtedly drive growth. But what's dangerous is that technology has fostered a lackadaisical environment, where we sit back and react and spend little time planning, or thinking about, the future. The technology itself is great – but our reaction to it isn't always.

"I think sometimes we just sit back and let the computers handle things and such. Maybe we're just too hands off as managers."
—Amanda, 29, Manager, Lincoln, NE

Poor Training – One of the most disturbing aspects of MBC has been the insights we've gained into America's business readiness, or lack thereof, while conducting focus groups. Specifically, in the course of our focus groups, we've found that many American managers simply lack the training for rigorous business management, and, consequently, are often slow to act.

As our economy has created millions of new jobs over the past twenty years, we've found that many managers lack **any** formal business training – much less an advanced degree or any sort of advanced academic training relating to management. Thus, it shouldn't really be that surprising that Americans embraced MBC so easily. Essentially, what we're saying is that many of our managers simply don't know any better.

> *"I think you can learn everything you need to know on the job...eventually."*
> —Cecile, 28, Manager, Jackson, MS

> *"A lot of our young managers learn everything on the job. Sure, they're inexperienced. But I think they eventually get to where they need to be."*
> —Dale, 52, General Manager, Portland, OR

Greed/Instant Gratification – As you'll recall from the opening chapter of this book, greed is a very powerful motivator. As we carefully argued in that opening chapter, many Americans simply don't want to wait to do the right thing in the long-term – they want as much reward as they can get **right now**.

This has become one of the major factors which underlie the MBC philosophy. Managers are focused on short-term risk and rewards, loathe acting on something that may pay off years from now.

And if you're thinking that this is the way business has always been, you're wrong. It took many years before *USA Today*, the nation's newspaper, broke even – much less before it made a profit. Clearly, the managers at this fine newspaper were managing for the long-term when they launched such initiatives as including color pictures and graphics, one major feature story in each of the paper's four main sections, and a national weather map. Many of these features are common today at newspapers all across the U.S., but were unheard of at the time *USA*

Today launched. If *USA Today* had been managed only for short-term gain, the paper surely would have looked different that it does today.

> *"We have to make our profit goal this quarter, no question.*
> *And that's not negotiable."*
> —Robert, 42, Manager, Santa Fe, NM

Laziness – One last key factor in the rise of MBC is a human factor – you know, one of those seven deadly sins, slothfulness.

After more than twenty-five years of economic growth interrupted by only two or three short recessions, our theory is that American workers have gotten somewhat fat and happy with prosperity. By historical standards, we've enjoyed relatively tranquil economic waters over the last quarter century, with relative peace in the world, stable energy prices (unlike the past year and the 1970's), and strong growth in democratic governments across the world. This has led to robust economic growth in the United States, which is once again (or still?) the world's top economy.

So let's face it — we're spoiled! If managers and workers are faced with three potential consequences to their actions – growth, robust growth, and eye-popping growth, we're sometimes going to opt for the most positive outcome with the least amount of risk. And that's MBC. We won't act until we know for sure what problems we're facing. And what's the harm? We're still growing our companies and our economy, aren't we?

> *"We may never have another recession again. The economy just*
> *chugs on."*
> —Dale, 48, Office Worker, Oakland, CA

"A good profit is almost guaranteed at our company."
—Tilde, 44, Office Manager, Garden Grove, CA

Summary: The Principles Of MBC

- When managing, always consider short-term goals, not long-term goals.

- Be reactive, not proactive.

- Don't worry about problems you can't really see today – the future will come soon enough.

- Technology can play a critical role in MBC – allowing managers to make decisions in a timely – i.e., last-second - fashion.

- Don't worry about formal job training – you can learn on the job.

- When in doubt, do nothing!

- Profits today are much more important than profits out in the future.

The Changing Work Place

"Choose a job you love," Confucius once wrote, "and you will never have to work a day in your life." It's fair to say that many of us work a whole lot of days in our lives, for we toil at jobs that are not particularly enjoyable or satisfying. Some really bad news out of our focus group work is that it certainly appears as if Americans are becoming **less satisfied** with their jobs over time.

> *"I hate my damn job. I think most workers do."*
> —Earl, 33, Truck Driver, Queens, New York

> *"My life would be great if I never had to work."*
> —Kit, 40, Clerk, Edison, NJ

In fact, a landmark study conducted in 1999 by David Blanchflower of Dartmouth College and a British counterpart, Andrew Oswald of the University of Warwick, found that workers older than their mid-30's in the U.S. had become significantly less satisfied with their work since the mid-1970's. In their study of industrial democracies, the two researchers found that Americans were also significantly less satisfied, overall, than workers in other parts of the free world.

This certainly fits the pattern we've observed over the past decade, of an American work force that is increasingly falling out of love with their jobs. The reasons for this dissatisfaction, from our focus group work, include:

- Long hours.
- Too much stress worrying about layoffs.
- Slim office staffs which have overburdened many workers.
- Not enough vacation time.
- A strong dislike of performance appraisal methods.
- Inadequate pay.
- Too much infighting on the job among staffers.
- Lack of good office etiquette.

Regardless of whether we love or hate our jobs, we know positively from focus group discussions that our work environment is **changing**. The American workplace is a dynamic environment, much like life itself, with more than 100 million workers and millions of different companies, from large conglomerates to sole proprietorships. Accordingly, the workplace is constantly changing and evolving. In fact, we'd go so far as to say that, even beyond MBC, the American workplace is being radically transformed.

My father was an executive for more than forty years during the latter half of the Twentieth Century. He probably wouldn't much recognize our contemporary work environment – my Dad would likely feel like a fish out of water if there was a "Bring A Parent To Work Day." (He's now happily retired.) Things have changed that much.

David Bowie once belted out, "Time may change me. But I can't trace time," in the song, *Changes*. Well, even if we can't trace time, we can definitely trace the major changes in the work place over the past several decades from focus group work, and they are outlined throughout the remainder of the chapter.

CHANGES TO THE WORK WORLD

Shrinking Leisure Time
The Blurring Of Work & Domestic Life
Promote Me Or Else! (Or I'll Sue!)
The Critical Importance Of Negative Word-Of-Mouth
The Information Age
A Skills-Challenged Work Force
The Rise Of "The Working Retired"

<u>Shrinking Leisure Time; Hello Mr. and Mrs. Workaholic</u> –
No doubt about it, we are just plain tired.

Despite the rapid growth in our standard of living over the past fifty years, Americans tell us that they spend far more time working than ever before, and less time on vacation. That's right – most Americans (of any and all age groups) tell us that they are working more now than at any point in their lives.

"It seems like all I ever do is work."
—Peter, 36, White Collar, Brookline, MA

"Work, work, work. That's all I do. I get up, I go to work. I get home late – 8 or 9 [o'clock] – kiss the kids good night, and then I crash. And that's my life."
—Pete, 56, Manager, Escondido, CA

Whether they are hourly wage earners or high-salaried white collar workers, the lament always sounds the same – too much work!

The reasons vary for our workaholism, from economic necessity to the strong work ethic of some contemporary workers. Regardless, we appear to be putting in very long hours on the job.

It's undoubtedly true that respondents in focus groups some times exaggerate their responses to questions, especially on something as noble as how hard they work as providers for their families. However, through in-depth discussions in which we've actually analyzed work days, hour by hour, minute by minutes, we're largely found that Americans **are** working long hours. Sure, we exaggerate a bit, but that doesn't change the overall picture. Americans clearly are exhausted by work – we're way overtired.

As a consequence, we're likely to see several emerging trends in the near-term:

- **Burn-out:** Some Americans will simply say they've had enough and are too tired to continue working. Accordingly, they will retire – some for the long-term, and some for anywhere from a few months to a year or two. Regardless, our expectation is that our labor force will shrink due to fatigue.

"I dream of taking some time off from work. Heck, even a month or two would be nice."
—Saul, 56, Retail Worker, Stamford, CT

"I'm in between jobs I guess. I've been off work for a few months, and I'm not really sure whether I'm going to go back, or what I'll do. I am just burned out and trying to re-charge the ol' batteries."
—Dick, 54, Unemployed/Retired, Kenosha, WI

- **Poor Health:** Health care costs are already skyrocketing, so how bad could a little upward jolt to health care costs really be? Tired, bedraggled American workers will continue to suffer everything from minor maladies (like colds and stomach problems) to major health problems in greater numbers. In effect, it's one of the prices we pay for our prosperity.

- **Mistakes On The Job:** This is the one major intangible to the "Tired America" trend. With battle fatigue will undoubtedly come lapses in judgment, some by top management at companies. But how many mistakes, and what types of mistakes, is largely yet to be determined. Undoubtedly, a rested work force would be far less likely to make critical mistakes. We can all cross our fingers and hope these future lapses in decision-making aren't critical or fatal.

The Blurring Of Work & Domestic Life – A second dramatic change in the American working life over the past twenty years is the blurring – or, rather, complete melding, of our work lives and our private lives. While at home on vacation, or when shopping with our family at the mall, we check e-mails, answer cell phones, and sometimes work on our laptops. And when at work, we shop (for personal items), buy tickets online, bid in online auctions and conduct other personal business. And we do it routinely.

> *"I think we all do personal business at work, don't we?"*
> —Dale, 27, Office Worker, Alpharetta, GA

> *"My wife, my friends, me, it seems like we're all doing a lot more work at home than we used to, even just a few years ago."*
> —Cindy, 41, Executive, Owings Mills, MD

The major impact of this trend is that it simply exacerbates our penchant for working long hours. Many readers will agree that hours seem to slip away while you're just doing a bit of paperwork, or returning a few e-mails at night or during a holiday weekend. Soon, it's past bedtime, and we're still working!

And while technology has enabled the "virtual office" to move wherever we are – the mall, a restaurant, at home in front of the TV – the down side is that it often feels as if we are chained to our work. It's as if an evil judge from the future (Judge Dredd?) has sentenced us to never leave work behind. We must seemingly go to work any time, anywhere.

Of course if this trend continues, we may be able to realize an ambition that myself and my co-workers espoused when we first entered the work force in the 1980's – to sleep on the job! If only technology some day allows us to work while we sleep…

Promote Me Or Else! – This trend should be headline news to anyone who has, or will, manage employees in the future, as it has major ramifications for **employers**.

> *"If I don't get a promotion or a fat raise every year, I'll just get a different job."*
> —Dale, 25, Sales Representative, Charleston, WV

This work trend, readily observed in focus groups, is the penchant or need for Americans to continually be promoted "up the ladder" at work, the sooner the better. And this trend is especially pronounced among younger workers, who seemingly have no problem ascending to the CEO's office before the tender age of 30, despite their relative lack of experience. To younger workers, this expectation seems quite natural and healthy. But this trend goes well beyond simple ambition. After all, ambition is one of the hallmarks of our entrepreneurial democracy. This trend is more like a compulsion, or an act of nature.

No, the current trend is, "Promote me, or else!" American workers now have a clear expectation that **every** job is a stepping stone, presumably to a higher paying, more powerful job. In other words, American workers aren't content to simply tread water by performing admirably in their current job, even if the rewards are relatively rich and/or they're satisfied with the job. No, their career must be on a rapid upward trajectory or ascendancy, or else they will find a new career path, and fast.

> *"If I don't get a promotion each year, I'll know I'm in a dead-end job."*
> —Sally, 24, Office Worker, Palo Alto, CA

This trend can have a profound impact on our economy in the near-term. **For starters, it certainly doesn't encourage loyalty**. No, to younger, modern workers, the only loyalty is to the career path. So expect a lot of job-hopping in the future.

This trend also seems inflationary, in nature. With each promotion, there's a corresponding pay raise. And we're talking about a world where companies often create titles, without a corresponding increase in responsibilities, merely to keep workers happy by offering a symbolic promotion. The bottom-line is that, with respect to pay, American workers are constantly churning for an increase.

Since workers are now conditioned, and have come to expect, promotions and pay raises on an almost continual basis, any bump in this road precipitates a profound increase in job dissatisfaction. **The bottom-line is that dissatisfied workers are typically less productive than happy workers.**

<u>**The Critical Importance Of Negative Word-Of-Mouth**</u> – This next change in the world of commerce applies largely to business owners, and the millions of customers who patronize their businesses. It has to do with what clever marketers have termed "word of mouth" – or what people have to say about you when they're "dishing."

When I was a young lad in college learning the "ABC's" of marketing, professors hammered home that if a customer had good things to say about your business – i.e., they were a satisfied customer – they'd tell three or four **other** people about your business. That, of course, is "positive" word-of-mouth.

But if they had negative things to say – the dreaded "negative" word-of-mouth – they might tell ten or more acquaintances about how lousy your business was. In other words, an unhappy customer will do a lot more damage than a happy customer can undo. So, even way back in the early 1980's, the message was clear: Be wary, be very wary, of the impact of negative word-of-mouth on the image and reputation of your business.

So guess what? Negative word-of-mouth has become even **more critical** in recent years. In our focus groups, we find that consumers take personal offense and respond in a virulent fashion to a negative experience (aided and abetted by blogs, of course). In other words, they just plain fume! And when they are crossed by a business, they want the whole world to know it! Consumers describe negative experiences in vivid detail, using colorful metaphors and graphic language. They may not remember their wedding day or their child's first birthday in much detail, but they sure remember every little detail about their negative experiences. Why, the recitations of these experiences in focus groups are so passionate, detailed and colorful that one can imagine throwing a party and awarding a door prize to the most horrible experience. (Based on the great stories we've heard, such a party might be a lot of fun!)

"They way they treated me was ridiculous. I won't relax until they close their doors."
—Alex, 26, Unemployed, Romulus, MI

"If they screw me, I will shout to everyone I know, until I die, to never go there for a meal again. That's how strongly I feel."
—Dean, 32, Teacher's Assistant, Elkhart, IN

But if the vivid detail of these negative encounters isn't bad enough for the offending business, the "half-life" of the negative experience may be worse. "Half-life" is a term that we've borrowed from physics and applied to the time it takes before a consumer begins to forget about a negative experience, the details of the experience, and before their passion subsides and the experience no longer takes up a large chunk of their "active memory." But the principle is much the same as the concept of "half-life" for a nuclear engineer. Whereas the "half-life" in physics refers to the time required for half the nuclei in a sample of a specific isotopic species to undergo radioactive decay, in business it's the time when the negative experience is still causing damage to the reputation and image of a business.

Without question, we've found lately that the "half life" for these negative word-of-mouth experiences is growing substantially, if not exponentially. In other words, consumers are holding onto their bitter, angry, vitriolic feelings and need to tell the world much longer than in the past.

The bottom line: Offend a customer at your own peril, for it may be the last time your business does it.

The Information Age – The advent of the Information Age has significantly influenced our economy for most of the last half of the 20th Century and the start of the 21st. We are quite literally awash in information at present; our ability to utilize the information already available is a far more vexing problem than our need to generate new information.

"Man, there is just so much data and information; it's everywhere, literally."
—Sal, 40, Financial Analyst, Boston, MA

How we're dealing with information is one of the biggest challenges and potential changes in the work place that we've observed in focus groups. I can summarize how Americans are responding to the Information Age, just within the last year or so, by noting:

We are much better at generating information than using it.

- Our ability to protect individual privacy in the midst of this information explosion is more questionable than ever. In the 2000's, Javelin Research & Strategy has released an annual fraud report estimating 4 million to 10 million I.D. thefts **per year in the United States**. That's an awful lot of privacy violations to be concerned about.

- Stress by American workers over information, everything from protecting privacy to the exponential increase in the quantity of information and how to deal with it, is having a negative impact on productivity. It has become so noticeable that we've coined a term in focus groups for this: "Information Stress Syndrome." It's basically a form of paralysis in which workers are so overcome with fear about dealing with information that they simply wash their hands of it and fail to act on the job – a variation on the old concept of Analysis Paralysis.

"We should be analyzing those customer records, but we just don't have the time or patience to deal with it. So we don't bother at all."
—Sherry, 38, Computer Technician, Plano, TX

"Our management is afraid we can't protect customer privacy, so they don't even let us analyze the data base, at all."
—Jim, 42, Analyst, Charlotte, NC

A Skills-Challenged Work Force – As noted earlier in this chapter, many contemporary American workers complain that they simply don't know what they're doing on the job. The American economy has been so successful at creating jobs – ten to twenty million new jobs per Presidential term – that we've essentially rushed a lot of novice workers to the front-line, with negative consequences for the economy.

> *"I sure wish I had gone to college. Then I might know what I'm doing."*
> —Bennie, 26, Administrative, New York, NY

> *"I wish I had paid more attention in college. I have no idea what I'm doing at work, to be honest."*
> —Salaam, 23, Administrative Assistant, Bronx, NY

So what can we do, either individually or as a society, to deal with, or enhance, a skills-challenged work force? Dr. Burgess' prescription for this problem is painfully simple, if not obvious: **education, education, education**. The idea of simply learning everything on the job is simplistic in business. It would not hurt to train even veteran workers in the intricacies of business. Think of it this way – it certainly couldn't hurt.

The Rise Of "The Working Retired" – We've come to know them well in our focus groups, and perhaps you do from your work environment, as well. Typically, they are middle-aged, pre-retirement (late 50's or early 60's). They tend to be veterans of the company. They've made some career advancement, but are no longer in line to be the "big boss." They're knowledgeable, but as much on matters of personnel, policy and politics as what the company really does.

> *"I'm just hanging on until retirement."*
> —David, 49, Marketing, Renton, WA

> "If I can hang on to get a pension, that's an accomplishment."
> —David, 50, Marketing, Minneapolis, MN

We've come to call them the "Working Retired" because of their career goal. They aren't working to advance up the corporate ladder, accumulate more power or influence, or even to set the world on fire.

And they're certainly not that interested in advancing the company's interests or moving the company ahead. No, they're interested in one thing, and one thing only. They want to hang on to their relatively high paying job until retirement.

And that's how they earned their name. In order to walk the tightrope toward retirement, they make little tangible contribution at work, eschewing political battles and sticky situations, as well as risky business gambits, so that they can simply hang on. They contribute as much (or as little) as a recent retiree. Yet, they're clearly still on the company payroll – that's why they're "working."

Think for a moment about your work situation, past or present. Without question, you probably know one or more Working Retired co-workers. From our focus groups, the Working Retired appear to be a sizeable segment of the population, numbering in the millions. With more Baby Boomers approaching retirement, this group is only going to mushroom in size.

As you can imagine, the Working Retired don't have a very positive impact on our economy. They draw full salaries, typically hefty middle to upper management salaries based on their many years of service. But they contribute very little to their employers, or to the economy as a whole in terms of output. In other words, they are a net drain on the economy.

So what can we do about this group as managers? Very little, actually. Clearly, the Working Retired are being rewarded, at least in part, for years of loyalty, so slicing them from the payroll is an unappealing option.

However, in a perfect world, management has a right to demand productivity from **everyone** drawing a salary or hourly wage. It's unconscionable to spend five, ten, or fifteen years at the back-end of a career simply hanging on. Certainly, older, accomplished workers must be handled with a modicum of care – but it's clear that American managers can't devote 10% or 20% of their payroll to workers simply waiting for their first Social Security check.

We encourage readers to share ideas with each other, and with the author, on how to handle the Working Retired situation in the future. But handle it we must.

"I don't do much at work. I just draw a salary."
—Leo, 58, Senior Executive, Pasadena, CA

The Age Of Exclusionary Marketing (And Why It's Not Working) — One of the most dramatic changes in our economy over the past twenty years is the invention and explosion of what we've come to call "Exclusionary Marketing." Permit me a moment to explain.

One of the basic tenets of modern marketing – and I should know, having earned a couple of degrees in the field and having sat through thousands of hours of lecture time – is that you need to target the right consumer with your message, product, and the rest of your marketing programs (what the industry calls the "marketing mix"). Now, what determines the "right" customer for a given product varies on a product by product basis. But the key to the targeting concept is that it is much more **economical** and **effective** to target select groups of current customers, rather than the whole world. For instance, it makes no sense to target consumers who have little income with ads and a marketing blitz for a luxury automobile. The car marketer is far more effective at targeting only upper income consumers – e.g., through buying ads on certain radio or TV stations, or buying a list for a direct mail campaign of upper income consumers.

For roughly fifty years or so, marketers have routinely used this "target marketing" strategy, with great success. But, like a body-builder on steroids, or a sport that's gone "extreme," target marketing has morphed into "Exclusionary Marketing."

Take, for instance, MTV or the major broadcast networks. They've worked hard to lure younger viewers with youth-oriented dating shows (*A Shot At Love With Tila Tequila* or *Next*) and reality shows, as well as new "stars" (such as Blake Lively or Leighton Meester) to headline shows like *One Tree Hill* (aimed at young viewers) with young adult music, dialogue, and themes. The bottom line is that there is no mistaking who the broadcast networks and MTV are targeting with these programs – teens, pre-teens, young adults, and anyone else under the age of twenty-five. The problem is that no one **over** the age of twenty-five would be caught dead watching these shows, or would ever **want** to watch one of these shows. And that's Exclusionary Marketing.

At its most basic, Exclusionary Marketing is targeting one group so well that you prevent any **other** group from wanting to use your product – like a TV show so beloved by pre-teens that no adult would understand, much less want to watch, the show. (You exclude groups other than your target market from consuming the product, intentionally or unintentionally.) And this just doesn't happen on TV, but with a spate of products. And it doesn't have to involve young adults, either. Try a role reversal, and think for a moment about a product so strongly identified with geriatrics that most other Americans don't want to use it (prunes, Exlax, Depends, er...you get the idea). We've taken the opportunity to list a few products below that are so strongly identified with their target that no one else is particularly interested in using the product.

> *"No way I would drive that car. It's for Seniors."*
> —Jim, 22, Student, Albany, NY

"I couldn't drive that car. That's kids stuff."
—Sam, 58, Bus Driver, San Francisco, CA

PRODUCT VS. TARGET

Mini-Vans →	Families
Classic Rock Stations →	Aging Baby Boomers
Murder She Wrote →	Seniors
Dance Clubs →	Young Adults
Hip-Hop →	Teens & Young Adults
I – Pod →	Teens & Young Adults
Anti Wrinkle Creams →	Young & Middle Age Women
Hair Removal →	Young & Middle Age Women
Cleaning Supplies →	Women
Automotive Supplies →	Men
Pickup Trucks →	Men
Avanza Markets →	Hispanics
Tools and Hardware →	Men
"Crotch Rocket"/Sports Bike →	Young Men

Okay, I know where you're heading. You're wondering what's wrong with this Exclusionary Marketing? Isn't it great to be so strongly identified with one target segment? To which I can answer emphatically, "No!"

The goal is to have your target identify with the product – **but not to alienate everyone else in the marketplace from wanting to try it.** When I was a child, ABC featured the original *Dating Game* and

Newlywed Game in prime time. These were hip shows clearly targeted at young adults – but watched by others, including older adults, Seniors, and even me! (I was only eight years old at the time – clearly not a young adult). Why, if these shows were on today and were taken over by Exclusionary Marketers, they'd feature swearing, nudity, lesbianism jokes and a lot of other material that would preclude anyone but a young adult from watching – and that's a shame.

When the Mustang automobile was launched in the 1960's, it was originally targeted at young adult males. However, research clearly showed that middle-aged males also loved the car, viewing it as a way to re-capture their lost youth. Mustang was a **huge** commercial hit for Ford Motor Company. However, if Ford had practiced today's Exclusionary Marketing at that time, they would have alienated the middle-aged drivers from being interested in Mustang, which would have severely limited the car's financial success. Ford knew that the key to success was to expand the market, not to exclude it.

In talks I give, I compare Exclusionary Marketing to the Super Bowl. Sure, the Super Bowl is targeted at pure football fans. But guess what? With colorful halftime shows, ground-breaking ads, visits by Hollywood stars and pre-game hype, the game isn't just enjoyed by pure football fans. No, it's watched by more than 100 million Americans every year, helping to sell millions in merchandise, precipitating millions in bets on the game, and a whole lot of "water cooler" talk at work. It's hardly just for hard-core football fans. Most of the time, that's how marketing should work. Sure, target your core audience, but don't limit people from outside the target from enjoying your product. Try to sell as many units or items as you can – like making the Super Bowl the biggest, most hyped game on the planet. That should be the true goal of marketing.

So let's hope that Exclusionary Marketing heads the same way as the dinosaurs soon – to extinction.   In a country that's already painfully divided (see Chapter 3), the last thing we need is to be divided so harshly by our marketing campaigns.

Chapter 5:

A Day In The Life –

Understanding Our

American Lifestyle

✫ ✫ ✫ ✫ ✫

"Life is like an onion. You peel it off one layer at a time, and sometimes you weep."
—Carl Sandberg

"Life can only be understood backwards; but it must be lived forwards."
—S.A. Kierkegaard

"I think my life is completely changed from ten years ago. Maybe even from five years ago. It just seems different in so many ways. It just seems so… what's the word? Um, fast! That's it, my life is just so sped up these days, so fast!"
—Jim, 44, Contractor, St. Louis, MO

When I was in high school, one of my favorite plays was Thornton Wilder's ***Our Town***. For those not familiar with the book, or those far removed from their high school lit classes and needing a bit of an update, ***Our Town***, written early in the 20th Century, is a short play about life in fictional, small-town America. The Pulitzer Prize-winning play tells the story of a seemingly unremarkable group of citizens from Grover's Corner, New Hampshire, living their unremarkable lives. Without spoiling the plot, the play is really a metaphor for our own daily lives, cleverly making the point that no matter how mundane, routine or uninteresting life may seem at times – even in a remote small town – life itself is precious. It gave me chills then, and it does now. What a message.

Believe it or not, *Our Town* is still inspirational to me, some thirty years later, even in my professional life. But professionally speaking, its message is slightly different. Sure, *Our Town* still reminds me that life itself is precious. But in much the same way that Wilder uses the seemingly unimportant daily lives of his characters to reveal key insights into their personalities and views on life, so also do our daily lives reveal much about America. No matter how mundane or routine our lives may seem, how we live, day by day, hour by hour, tells so much about how we Americans think and live or, in colloquial terms, what we're really all about. And if one truly wants to understand America early in the 21st Century – and that's really the major point of this book – then one must understand the American lifestyle, circa 2008-2009.

One way to understand our lifestyle in this country would be to assign a private detective to shadow each of us twenty-four hours a day, seven days a week. Why, the detective profession would immediately rise to a prominence not seen since 1970's detective shows like *Mannix, Cannon* and my personal favorite, Jim Garner in the *Rockford Files*.

Alas, the detective scheme isn't practical. There are about 300 million Americans now, so there aren't nearly enough detectives to track all of us. And who would pay for the detective work? Any serious student of TV detective shows knows that an earnest gumshoe will run hundreds of dollars per day, plus expenses.

So if we're to understand how Americans live, the next best thing is our focus groups. (You probably knew that this is where we were headed!) We've spent literally thousands of hours talking to Americans about everything from the most mundane details of their daily lives to those seminal moments that define their lives, so it's actually not that difficult to paint a portrait, and a detailed one at that, about how we live.

But beyond a detailed description of how we live, this chapter will really focus on what's **changing** about how Americans live, or where we're headed as a country. We Americans have never been much for standing still or jogging in place. No, we are constantly changing and evolving, as we react to the world around us, and as we try to shape and change the world around us into the world in which we want to live.

"I think things are a lot different than when I was a kid, for sure."
—Jan, 28, Secretary, Deland, FL

"My life has changed, even in the last few years."
—Sanford, 22, Student, Atlanta GA

Life, as we know it, is complex. There are the small, mundane occurrences which mark our daily lives – you know, "Don't sweat the small stuff." In contrast, life is also comprised of once-in-a-lifetime events, such as marriage or having children, as well as somewhat sporadic, infrequent events, such as buying a car. It's all part of life, from the routine to the truly unique and special.

So, as you might expect, our lives are so complex and detailed as to warrant **two** chapters in this book on the American lifestyle. The first will focus on specific aspects of **daily** life that are changing, from what we eat to how we sleep. The second chapter focuses on those aspects of the American lifestyle that aren't daily or frequent occurrences in our lives, but sporadic, infrequent, and sometimes truly special events – e.g., for many, marriage is a once-in-a-lifetime occurrence, and yet it's one of the most critical influences on our lifestyle, or how our lives turn out.

So climb aboard as we take a detailed look at the changing American lifestyle. Some things you may recognize, and others may surprise you. Regardless, when these two chapters are finished, you should have a much clearer vision as to what America is really like and, more importantly, where it's headed.

> *"But it's just another day. It's just another day."*
> —John Mellencamp in the song, *"Just Another Day"*

Our Daily Lives

We're going to start our magical mystery tour (with apologies to the Beatles) of the American lifestyle by examining the components of our daily lives. And, as a reminder, we're focusing more on those aspects of the American lifestyle that have changed, or are currently changing, as this will help us to focus in on where we're headed as a country.

Busy, Busy, Vroom, Vroom – Without question, the most universal change in American lifestyles over the past decade is the pace of our lifestyles. Ask any group about their lives, and invariably the answers are pretty much in sync with:

> *"I'm always on the go."*
> —Jill, 32, Housewife, Orange, CA

> *"I'm busy. Man, I'm so busy that I can't ever remember when life slows down.*
> —Paulie, 44, Rental Car Clerk, Hyde Park, NY

> *"Get out of my way, people, cause I'm going a mile a minute. Yeah, I am terribly busy, I admit it."*
> —Sandy, 40, Sales Representative, Albany, NY

Another one of the early lessons at Focus Group Moderator Training School is that you can never draw statistical conclusions out of a small focus group, especially when all the respondents have the ability to influence one another. (That's called bias.) Fair enough. But with apologies to the Lords of Focus Groups, I can tell you that about 99.9% of the people in our focus groups over the past decade have claimed to be busy – not kind of busy, but "your hair is on fire," get-out-my-way busy.

Far be it from us to doubt the words of our loyal focus group respondents, but…we don't believe Americans are nearly as busy as they say. Why would we doubt them? Well, for starters, we hear this same claim about being busy from **everybody**, from the CEO of a major corporation (yes, they come to focus groups, too), all the way to high school students on summer break and the unemployed. Yes, we've had literally hundreds of unemployed respondents through the years tell the moderator that they are **so** busy. (They usually can't recall what they're so busy with, but they know that they're busy.)

"Man, I haven't had a free hour in so long. Life is just kicking me in the ass, really."
—Don, 24. Student, Erie, PA

Second, when we press people from all walks of life in the focus groups to tell us **why** they're so busy and exactly what they do all day long, we often hear silence. Even allowing somewhat for the "stage fright" of discussing your life in a group full of strangers, the silence on this issue is deafening.

So why are Americans not exactly telling the truth about being so busy? Why are they lying?

Well, they're not. Hang with me while I explain.

Americans are busy, amazingly so. You know it, I know it, we all know it. Our lives are crammed with activities, we work far too much, we sleep very little (at least by historical standards), and we are literally on the run at times, from appointment to appointment, from dawn until bedtime. This isn't made up – it's documented by many sources. For instance, in 2005, the *New York Times*, the *Families and*

Work Institute and Dr. Edward Hallowell all documented in major publications and studies how busy Americans really are.

We're probably just not as busy as we sometimes think. In focus groups, when we work with respondents to break down their daily lives into component parts, we often find many hours per week that are wide open and unbooked – several hours before bedtime, the dinner hour, lunch time, to name but a few. Plus, we know that we Americans do vacation, we do take days off, and some of us are not working. (According to the U.S Bureau Of Labor Statistics, the unemployment rate in America has fluctuated between 5% and 7% since 1960.)

So are Americans seriously delusional about the pace of modern life? Not at all. Our focus group work has shown that we really **do** feel super-busy, all the time. Even when we're on vacation or unemployed, we have a giant "honey do" list which makes us feel swamped. Before bed, we don't relax and enjoy TV all the time. Often, we return e-mails on the computer and ponder the next day at work. Even when we're home "relaxing," how many hours are spent on home repair, home remodeling and other serious jobs? Indeed, the pace of modern life is **so** fast, compared to just a generation ago or even ten years ago, that we feel like we've living life at supersonic speeds, all the time.

"Sunday isn't a day or rest. It's probably my busiest day of the week."
—Delford, 44, Handyman, Jacksonville, FL

"Man, with kids and work, there isn't ever a day when I don't feel dog tired when I get to bed at night. Ever."
—Jill, 39, Administrative Assistant, Bloomington, MN

Our perception of the pace of life has most certainly merged into our reality. Even when the "caution flag" of life is flying at the race track, we're driving 200 or 300 miles per hour, at least in our minds.

"Zoom, zoom, zoom," might not just be a commercial ditty from a car commercial, but the theme song to our lives.

At some point, we may relent and return to a more modest pace in America, if only to prolong and enhance the quality of our lives. We actually expect this to happen, incrementally, over the next decade or two. But in the meantime, what can we expect?

The Impact Of Our Busy Lifestyles

1. **Health care costs will soar during the next decade.**

2. **American life expectancy will decline.**

3. **More time-saving products will hit the market.**

4. **Vacation related and leisure product sales will explode.**

5. **A major sales increase in sleep/nocturnal-related products will occur.**

---

1) Eventually, the crazy pace of our lives and the stress connected to that pace will have serious consequences on our health. **We expect health care costs — already rapidly accelerating – to soar even further in the next decade.**

2) **With our sagging health, American life expectancy may fall –** and significantly – for the first time in decades.

3) **Time-saving products and** devices **– from food to transportation – will find huge markets**. I am not a scientist, but someone creating a "transporter," as seen on *Star Trek*, to move us around the planet on a molecular basis, seems unlikely. (Imagine what a GREAT time-saver that would be!) But food

that enters the bloodstream without being digested or swallowed seems likely – e.g., a gourmet meal in a pill or a "shot" of food. And transportation devices that help us navigate the planet rapidly– anyone test driven a hover car that floats in space, or a bullet train that can break the sound barrier? – seem likely. All in all, innovations that save time have the greatest chance for commercial success in the second decade of the century, if not beyond.

> *"Man, if you can get me from Point A to Point B faster, or with less wear and tear, that would be huge."*
> —Sam, 58, Sales Executive, Plano, TX

4) Eventually, this pace will wear us out. But not yet, apparently. **In the meantime, expect sales of vacation-related and leisure products to explode.** Sure, part of the problem is that we are always working and never have time for fun. But with the rapid pace of our lives, we will simply need more vacation and leisure-time pursuits to sustain us. And expect at least some of these products to fit into our busy daily routines as well – e.g., the ability to watch a movie through our sub-conscious while we are working at our computers.

5) **Finally, one big growth sector in the next decade will be our nocturnal pursuits – no, not what you're thinking, but sleeping-related products.** As we sleep less each decade, the quality of our sleep will need to increase to compensate, both physically and mentally. My company expects a whole new category of sleeping-related products to emerge into what we call "power sleeping." We may not sleep very much any more, but when we do, our expectations will be sky-high for the rest and comfort of the sleep. So expect new products in categories

such as sleeping furniture, sleepwear, sleep accessories, and even sleeping nutrition. Personally, I am looking for some type of product that will allow us to work and sleep simultaneously. Oh, if only they could have invented that before I attended all those college lectures!

"Man, when I was younger, I used to fantasize about who I'd sleep with. I still fantasize about sleeping, but it's always just by myself in a nice comfy bed, with no kids or wife bothering me."
—Derek, 38, Retail, Jefferson City, MO

Our Changing Lifestyles

Beyond the rapid pace of modern American living, we've also observed and discussed several other major emerging changes in our daily lifestyle with focus group respondents.

Emerging Changes in Our Daily Lifestyle

Long Commutes

Meals Together? (Forgettabout It!)

You're So Fat You Could...

ZZZZZZZZZ

$4.00 Gasoline, Oh My!

Alone Again, Naturally

You've Got...

Long Commutes – Whether in planes, trains or automobiles (to borrow a phrase from the movies), Americans are spending more time than ever commuting to their jobs daily.

"Sometimes I feel like I spend more time commuting to work than I do actually working on the job."
—Jerry, 34, Graphic Arts, Portland, OR

A decade or so ago, there were widespread predictions that Americans would largely telecommute in the future; that is, work at home and essentially connect to their employer electronically, through the Internet, cell phones and the like. Alas, the prediction was wrong.

It ignored the "human factors" related to working – namely, that people largely enjoy interacting with other human beings while working. True, working at home has many advantages, but the work environment is hard to simulate anywhere but at work. Thus, most Americans still commute to a job, many in central cities (large metro areas) after a daily jaunt from the suburbs.

"Working at home every once in a while is okay. But that's as often as I can do it. No way could I do it all the time."
—Steph, 30, Statistician, Dulles, VA

Our commute times have increased dramatically in recent years. By February of 2004, the U.S. Census Bureau sent out a press release announcing that New York City residents spent nearly one week per year, on average, simply commuting to their jobs, and residents of Chicago, Philadelphia and Riverside, CA were spending nearly thirty minutes per day, on average, commuting to work. The reasons for this significant increase are fairly straightforward:

1) We are moving further and further from the city in our quest to find new, largely undeveloped (and affordable) suburbs in which to live.

2)   Traffic and congestion have worsened considerably as our country has topped the 300 million population mark. Even if we're still living in the same house after all these years, it simply takes longer for most of us to make our way into the central city. or even to most suburbs.

So be prepared to spend more time in cars, trains and buses, listening to the radio as you inch along to work. It's simply taking longer to get there.

While the merits of American spending, collectively, billions of hours of idle time each day commuting are debatable, this phenomenon offers tremendous opportunity to business – a captive audience of daily commuters, just waiting to be reached with content and advertising.

The obvious solution to this is drive-time radio, right? You know, endless time spent on commercials, occasionally interrupted by a song or an amusing (more likely, embarrassing) personal anecdote by the DJ, with news at the top of the hour. Unfortunately, this format hasn't changed much in ten, er, twenty, er, thirty, er...well, for as long as I've been alive. So the challenge for marketers is to reach the large audience of drive-time commuters, whether through radio, billboards, or new digital media, with more compelling content and messages. And the very same could be said for all those commuters on trains, buses or other forms of transportation.

"I'd give anything to have something to do while sitting in the car each day, as long as it didn't compromise safety."
—John, 55, Executive, Indianapolis, IN

"Man, that time on the train is just plain wasted each day. I sure as hell wish I could make it more productive."
—Jerry, 29, Teacher, Bronx, NY

Meals Together? Forget It – When I was young, a favorite show – as it was for many kids who grew up in the '60's or '70's – was *Leave It To Beaver*. Beyond the cloying cuteness of the lead, Jerry Mathers as The Beav, what made the show so compelling was the idyllic lifestyle of the Cleavers. You know, Mom in a dress with pearls, dusting daily…Dad constantly reading the newspaper, oblivious to the emergence of that radical new thing called the TV…and nightly meals together, complete with a water glass, fine china and exquisite silver, just like in a restaurant. Well, wake me from that nightmarish world at any time.

But eating dinner together each night seems positively quaint, at least for the 90% of American families (we estimate) who eat meals "on the run" these days. Yes, a distinct change in our American lifestyles is that we no longer dine together nightly. So what, you say?

"I can't remember the last time we had dinner together."
—Stevie, 28, Municipal Worker, Overland Park, KS

"I don't know if we've ever had family dinners together, like when I was a kid. Can't remember when."
—Cecil, 40, Teacher's Assistant, Augusta, ME

Instead of group meals each night – forget the water glasses for a moment – the pattern we observe is that women are typically charged with feeding younger children, to ensure the nutritional content of their food. For all of the other family members, from teenagers engaged in extracurricular activities to males coming home from work, meals are "forage for what you can find." In other words, they are rather informal, and, in all likelihood, **solitary.**

And that's why meal time has changed our lifestyles. In *Leave It To Beaver* times, dinner (the evening meal) was our best chance to communicate with each other, from family issues to personal problems.

Beyond the caloric intake, dinner time was our family socializing session.

As you can imagine, in a world in which many household members eat meals on the fly – heck, many of us don't ever see other family members when they're eating – we no longer communicate much with each other, either. We believe that this has strongly eroded family cohesion, leading to a host of behavioral and psychological problems for some, including, we believe, the increase in the American divorce rate. (According to the U.S. Census Bureau, about 50% of all U.S. marriages still end in divorce.) As Martha Stewart might say, this is **not** a good thing.

"It seems like I never see my kids any more, much less talk to them."
—Dolly, 55, Housewife, Shaker Hts., OH

"We always try to have meals together, but it just never seems to work out. But it sure would be nice."
—Alex, 56, Administrative, Queens, NY

And this is where technology might help us turn back the clock. True, we might not ever return to the "family dining hour" featured on early TV sit-coms. But we have seen the emergence of tools that, at least theoretically, can help us to communicate more effectively with each other and help maintain family cohesion – like cell phone plans for the family, joint/family calendars on the computer, and PDA devices like blackberries.

We believe that this is but the tip of the iceberg in terms of tools and technology to enhance communications, because of the importance of maintaining a strong family unit. We'd probably all agree that families which converse, and which enjoy some family activities together, are more likely to be happy, healthy family units. So in the future, look for innovations such as **voice-activated devices to inject the** personalities of missing family members into dinner conversation, products which project the images of missing family members into meals, robotics, and even **changes in meals, food preparation and food products which aid family cohesion.**

"I sometimes feel that I flat-out miss my own kids. And that's a shame."
—Sally, 46, Housewife, Ballwin, MO

You're So Fat You Could... – Remember this old series of jokes? MTV even had a show built around it. Whatever the subject, the joke was always the same: "You're so FILL IN THE BLANK, you..." You can fill in your own punch line here.

Unfortunately, there's no nice way to say this, but America is fat. Really fat. Most reliable estimates peg the really fat proportion of the population – the clinically obese – at 40% of all Americans. Add in the percentage that are five or ten pounds overweight, and it boggles the mind.

The goal here is not to judge any of us Americans for what we weigh, or don't weigh. Rather, it's simply to acknowledge that one of the biggest changes to the American lifestyle in recent years is that many of us spend years waddling our way through life. If Americans were animals, we've moved from being a jaguar or leopard to being a top-heavy penguin.

"I know I've put on twenty or thirty pounds in recent years. I'd guess that most people my age have."
—Enrique, 38, Laborer, Los Angeles, CA

"It seems like I just gain two or three pounds every month. And before you know it, you're fifty pounds overweight."
—Sylvain, 50, Executive, Southfield, MI

Beyond the jokes about weight, some of the consequences of our collective heft are easy to discern. For instance, we Americans dine out an awful lot, compared to just a generation ago. New restaurant concepts and new styles of cuisine continue to boom. (We've done focus groups for many new restaurant concepts over the past twenty years.) Interest in food preparation and cooking remains high, as well as in new grocery store products. We even have a major cable TV network devoted to food, and nothing but food. (Thank you Emeril!)

Another unfortunate, but easy to discern, impact of our size is the increase in health care costs. A fatter population is thought to be less healthy (e.g., with respect to cardiac care) and costs much more to maintain. Hence, health care costs have soared, and are expected to continue soaring.

As for less noticeable side effects to our collective weight affliction, check out the seats on an airplane. Why, they aren't nearly wide enough for some plump Americans. But they can't remove a whole row of seats in an industry starved for revenue. And it's impractical to widen multi-million dollar airplanes crafted from steel and aluminum.

America's ballooning waistlines have had, and will continue to have, a dramatic impact on what we buy. Stretch pants and mumus are in, fitness equipment and jogging shorts are out. That's merely one example of the many and varied changes due to our size. Regardless, America is definitely fat – but are we happy, too?

> *"I look at pictures of myself when I was thin, and I'd just like to cry now. It doesn't even look like me, now."*
> —Dorey, 72, Retired, Wausau, WI

Zzzzzzzzzz – In focus groups, our respondents complain that they are just plain tired. No, not tired of the focus groups (though this might be understandable), but tired, in general. In fact, fatigue has become one of the most common American maladies, impacting literally millions of Americans.

We **do** sleep an awful lot less than we used to. In fact, an article by Robert Roy Britt in *Live Science* claims that we sleep even less than we think we do these days, barely more than six hours per night. As one might expect, given the rapid pace of modern American living previously discussed, who can sleep with all this excitement around us? As per the old saying, you snooze, you lose.

> *"I just don't have time to sleep like I used to. I wish I did, but it's just not in the cards."*
> —Rafel, 36, Teacher, Chicago, IL

> *"Sleeping would be nice. I always feel tried. But who's got time?"*
> —Mary, 50, Housewife, Kansas City, KS

But beyond the rabbit's pace to our lives, we also find in our focus group discussions that sleep is simply passé. Yes, it's just not cool to sleep, for several reasons:

For men, sleep is sometimes associated with being somewhat weak or effeminate – i.e., only wimps sleep.

Many American heroes and icons have touted their lack of sleep in recent years, often with pride – from Donald Trump to Martha Stewart and Jay Leno. Of note, they aren't complaining of sleeplessness being a malady or serious health problem, but just a fact of life. And, as successful as they've been – think of Trump's millions or Martha Stewart's myriad of recipes – millions of Americans want to copy their waking ways.

Our standard for sleep has decreased. Forty years ago, eight to nine hours a day of sleep was considered the minimum for good health and wellness. Now, eight hours of sleep per night is definitely a luxury, like breakfast in bed. Talk to younger Americans, and many insist that five or six hours of sleep per night is all that's required.

There are definite consequences to the bleary-eyed America of the early 21st Century. And they start with productivity. On one hand, Americans work longer hours, and are awake more hours per day, week and month – and can certainly accomplish more than in the past when we were tucked into bed at least one-third of the time.

On the other hand, Americans may be accomplishing less these days when they are awake, simply because we're so tired at times. From slurred speech to foggy thinking and impaired reactions, we've all seen people who should have been in bed hours ago.

American productivity has steadily increased in recent years due, according to most economists, to the impact of the computer and other technology. We genuinely have to wonder if productivity increases will continue at the same pace as the last decade as we Americans get progressively more tired.

As we get more tired, we undoubtedly will need more time off from the job – be it sick days, vacation days, or even leaving work early. We've noted from focus group discussions in recent years that Americans tend to book-end holidays by taking additional time off, presumably because we are so tired and in need of a break. We've also noted that we tend to head home early from work on the days preceding three-day weekend holidays and even just plain Fridays at work – again, because we're just plain tired of working.

"I take every opportunity I can to be home with my family."
—Rachel, 37, Chef, Manhattan, NY

"Jeez, if we can get out of work, this place [of work] empties out in a big hurry."
—Robin, 40, Economist, Glen Falls, NY

Beyond time off and productivity, many focus group respondents have told us that they are simply more accident and illness prone these days because we are just so tired. We're heard chilling accounts of car accidents while driving home from work, or while going to pick up kids. And many Americans simply complain of illnesses, from headaches to the flu, that they ascribe to chronic fatigue.

In the 1950's, the Chordettes struck gold by singing the song "Mr. Sandman," including the immortal lines: "Mr. Sandman, bring us, please, please, please, Mr. Sandman, bring us a dream." It's not clear if Americans will once again develop a crush on ol' Mr. Sandman any time soon. In the meantime, who's up for watching reruns of Jimmy Kimmel followed by an old movie on cable, and maybe an infomercial? Thought so.

$4 Gasoline, Oh My! – In truth, this section probably could have been included with the next chapter of the book. After all, we don't exactly fill up the tank daily. But we do drive almost daily. And, as this book went to press, the huge surge in gasoline prices over the past two years is probably exerting the greatest change on our lifestyle of any single factor we've observed in our focus groups.

Americans are of two minds with respect to gasoline prices, and neither is exactly what's needed to meet this crisis head on, much less solve it.

On the one hand, many Americans have told us in focus groups that they are **not** impacted by gasoline at $4 per gallon or higher. Sure, they express concern and claim that they are more careful in their driving habits. However, upon discussing the issue in greater depth, it's clear that they've made very few changes to their driving habits. Not only can they afford gas at $4 to $5 per gallon, they simply don't want to take any time to change their driving habits.

"My life is good the way it is. I'm not going to give up the car or anything."
—Paula, 60, Executive, Nashville, TN

"Sure, gas is expensive. But it [$4 gas] hasn't changed my habits or anything."
—Jimmy, 68, Retired, Moline, IL

Conversely, the second group is the "sky is falling group." I don't want to be disrespectful of those Americans who truly can't afford gasoline at $4 to $5 or more per gallon. They have my deepest sympathies, as gas is essential to the American way of life. Instead, the "sky is falling group" can probably afford the gas, but is simply losing their heads in the midst of this modern energy crisis. In other words, they are in full panic mode.

With this group have come some serious behavioral changes. What belies these behavioral changes is the belief that the historic spike in energy prices is almost tantamount to nuclear war, a phenomenon that will ruin the American way of life.

"When gas is that high, you have to change the way you live. If you don't, it's pretty irresponsible."
—Janie, 49, Part-Time Worker, Missoula, MT

"This is a crisis, a catastrophe. We all have to change now."
—Parm, 40, Sale Representative, Carson, CA

"I think we will all live like cavemen in about one hundred years. There won't be any fossil fuels left by then."
—Harvey, 39, Technician, San Ramon, CA

As you can see from the respondent quotes accompanying this section, this group is truly in a major panic over the surge in energy costs, perhaps unnecessarily so. Sure, the increase in pump prices is clearly bad, and may cause a recession and some inflationary pressure on our economy in future years. But that's really all it is – a huge price spike in our commodities prices, roughly akin to the price of corn or wheat doubling. Beyond that, there are no real supply problems at this point (though the economies of China and India continue to consume petroleum in record amounts); we have as much gas as we need. In fact, the American way of life is hardly threatened, just a bit more expensive these days.

"It's put a dent in my pocketbook. But that's all the increase in gas prices has really done, when you get down to it."
—Thomas, 46, Clerk, Omaha, NE

"In history, this gas thing will be no big deal."
—Pamela, 50, Engineer, West Valley, UT

As noted earlier, this second group has modified some of its behavior (or lifestyle) in response to the soaring pump price:

- They are more likely to ride rapid transit, especially to work.
- They claim to be riding bicycles more often for neighborhood jaunts.
- Many are interested in hybrid cars or fuel-efficient economy cars. (They do still make those, don't they?), though few have actually purchased one.

And this last point is worth noting. American consumers have traditionally been very fickle, at least attitudinally, about energy costs, but have done very little to change consumption patterns over time, at least over the last fifty years. As soon as prices subside a bit, Americans traditionally lose interest in energy-savings, especially when it costs money. We tend to do the easy things that won't/don't change our lives and don't cost us money, like keeping tires inflated properly or turning off the lights in our house. But ask Americans to sacrifice or make a profound change to their lifestyles, like giving up a V-6 for a little economy car? Don't think so.

However, we believe that this energy crisis is different, if for no other reason than the environmental movement is in full bloom across America (and will be discussed later in this book), and is encouraging some Americans to cut back on energy consumption as part of the global warming issue. Plus, there is no indication that costs will subside any time soon. Sure, many analysts feel that oil is overpriced, but the market has been a one-way street for most of the last few years – up, up and away.

But ultimately, we believe that the majority of Americans will **not** be impacted by $4 or $5 per gallon gasoline, and will not change their lifestyles in response. This group is rather fond of the American lifestyle, and the price surge is largely considered an inconvenience, not a radical change.

> *"If gas costs $10 per gallon, it won't change my life at all."*
> —Boyd, 22, Student, Tucson, AZ

> *"No matter how much gas costs, my life will pretty much be the same."*
> —Alyson, 40, Writer, Littleton, CO

So gasoline at $5 per gallon is a disturbance or a distraction, but not a full-scale crisis for most Americans. At least so far.

Alone Again, Naturally – In the 1950's, American families ate dinner together and then retired to the family room to…watch TV together. Oh, how times have changed!

We don't spend so much time together any more. As we noted, we don't dine together each night, and we certainly don't watch TV together at night. In fact, we do just the opposite. In focus group after focus group, we've been told that most American families break into solo units to watch TV – that is, we each go to a different room, and watch TV by ourselves.

The obvious reason for doing so, in comparison to the 1950's, is that most households have far more than three channels worth of programming; some of us have hundreds of channels to choose from. So we divide up at night in order to find something for each of us to watch.

While this pattern may have helped TV ratings, it's unquestionably hurt family cohesion. Respondent after respondent in focus groups – mostly middle-aged parents – have told us how they lament disunity when it comes to American family leisure time. We simply don't spend much, if any, time together.

"I wish the kids would spend time with us some nights."
—Bristol, 32, Actress, Los Angeles, CA

"At night, it's not like we're even part of the same family. Everyone just goes off into their own direction and does their thing."
—Valerie, 44, Advertising, Bloomfield Hills, MI

"It seems like we all like different things [on TV], so we just go off to our own rooms each night to watch."
—Dave, 36, Unemployed, Richmond, VA

But beyond the social impact, solo TV viewing has spurred the sales of individual entertainment devices that are largely designed to be used by one user at a time. MP3 players, iPods and tiny portable TVs and other devices have flourished in recent years.

We're still a bit amazed that the TV industry doesn't market TVs for individuals, and not rooms. Like cell phones. Each TV could have different styling components and features, depending upon the owner/user. And they could be made more transportable, so we could watch it in different rooms of the house. But, like cell phones, it sure seems like we all deserve our own individual TVs.

Which makes us wonder, does the family that views apart, come apart? Only time will tell.

You've Got... – In the 1990's, millions of Americans logged onto the Internet and were greeted by AOL's famous phrase, "You've got mail!"

AOL's influence has since waned; but millions of Americans still log onto the Internet each night, viewing everything from e-mail to news headlines to porn. (There are more than one billions users of the web worldwide.)

In fact, the last major change in American lifestyles over the past decade outlined in this chapter is our increasing devotion to the cyber world. Part of the reason that we no longer watch TV together is that many of us are watching a computer screen each night, instead of the boob tube. But whether it's a computer screen or a TV screen, does it really matter?

Absolutely. In our focus groups, we've identified several major changes as to how Americans live, due directly to the Internet. And a warning – they're not all good changes, either.

1) **We're more isolated, and have less social interaction than ever.** Beyond telecommuting to work, which is slowly growing in popularity, many Americans simply find there is no/little need to interact with friends and relatives, not when they have the Internet offering 24/7 access to the world.

"I don't have to socialize much. I just live through the Internet."
—Jonnie, 38, Truck Driver, Salt Lake City, UT

"With all the stuff available online, I just don't hang out much with family or friends any more. It's just not necessary."
—Pacey, 26, Student, Long Island, NY

2)	**American Internet ethics tend to lag behind our traditional, real-world ethics.** Online, Americans tell us that they think nothing of plagiarizing material, of spreading malicious lies and rumors, or of watching pornography or reading salacious content. Of course, none of these behaviors would have been accepted in the real world ten years ago. But the anonymity of the Internet has emboldened many Americans, and it makes us wonder if Internet ethics will eventually supplant our traditional ethics in the U.S.

"I'm pretty anonymous when I'm online, so I can do anything I want, pretty much. Even if it's illegal. No one will catch me."
—Ahmet, 32, Student, Pasadena, CA

3)	**One unanticipated consequence to our frequent time online is our expectations with respect to timeliness and convenience.** An Internet world where users largely need only to type in a query to Google before receiving their information/content has begun to influence our sense of timing in every day life. In an odd twist, we've actually had respondents cite the speed of the Internet as a reason for being dissatisfied with:

- The speed of customer service at pharmacies.
- The speed of service at banks.
- The speed of cooking time and service at restaurants.

In short, whether we like it or not, the widespread use of the Internet is changing our views and expectations of many other aspects of life. Today, it's our expectations for timing; we anticipate that tomorrow it could be the acceptance of porn as commonplace/normal, or even the legalization.

Conclusion

There is an old saying in Colorado: If you don't like the weather, wait five minutes, and it will change. Well, the same is true for our lifestyle. It's forever changing, and rapidly at that. Beyond the rapid pace of modern American living, we've also observed that, at its most basic, our lifestyle is literally who we are. So if you're not sure that you like who you are, wait five minutes or so...

Chapter 6:

Life, She Is A Mother******

☆ ☆ ☆ ☆ ☆

"There will be two dates on your tombstone, and all your friends will read 'em. But all that's gonna matter is that little dash between 'em."
—Kevin Welch

"The best way to describe my lifestyle? That I live, I guess."
—Erskine, 46, High School Coach/Teacher, Brooklyn, NY

I have a confession to make. While starting to write this chapter, the second half of the book's focus on the American lifestyle, I went to the movies. No, not to see **Old School**, one of the greatest comedies ever, from which the chapter title is lifted – that would have been too much irony. No, as I munched popcorn and enjoyed the cool blast of air conditioning at my local cine-plex, I hunkered down into my "stadium" seat and started thinking about the best and worst movie roles during my lifetime.

The best roles? How about Billy Crystal in **When Harry Met Sally**, Christopher Reeve as **Superman**, or any movie starring Meryl Streep. (Yes, in my humble opinion, she's **that** good.)

But it's far easier for me to pick the worst role of all-time. Now, I'm not talking about a bad movie, a poorly written part, or even a bad actor. No, I'm thinking a **role** that would make me uncomfortable if, somehow, I was magically chosen to star in that movie tomorrow. It's not close...the hands down winner is Albert Brooks in **Defending Your Life.**

Okay, okay. The movie's a bit obscure. It was a hit when released, but is it a classic? For those not familiar with the movie, or readers who may have forgotten about Brooks' classic role, he plays a middle-aged man who's died quite suddenly in a car accident. After death, he's transported to Judgment City, a beautiful place somewhere in the cosmos where earthlings are sent to see if they've lived virtuous lives. If they have, they're sent on to some other plane of existence – heaven, perhaps? – and if not, they're sent **back** to earth to start a new life until they get it right. For a week, Brooks must "defend" his life at a trial in Judgment City. (I'm already squirming, thinking about how that would feel if I was playing Brooks' part.)

The defense of Brooks' life consists of watching various aspects of his life on a video screen in front of a three-judge panel, with a "prosecutor" pointing out the flaws in his life, and another attorney to defend the virtue. Ultimately, the judges will decide whether he advances onward or returns to earth. And that's the part that absolutely makes my skin crawl. Can you imagine the pressure? Can you imagine how you'd feel reviewing various aspects of your life – your future riding on the outcome - on a giant video screen in front of judges, lawyers, and courtroom visitors?

Yet, that's essentially our task in this chapter – to review our lives. No, not our everyday life, which we covered in depth in the preceding chapter. No, we want to examine those aspects of the American lifestyle that aren't regular, frequent, or even commonplace – those moments that would appear on the giant video screen if we were Albert Brooks. You know, things like:

Changes To Our Lifestyle

How we feel about terrorism

The role of kids in our society

The rise of "reality" TV

Our penchant for retiring early

Why and how we've become a nation of collectors

The rise of internationalism

Like Brooks in ***Defending Your Life***, we're going to focus on critically important aspects of our lives, how they're changing, and why. Fortunately, there isn't a set of judges to evaluate our lives and determine our eternal future, no video screen on which to view life's frustrations and failures, at least I don't **think** there is…

The Critical Side Of Life

We Have Nothing To Fear, Except…Everything! - Without question, terrorism, and the threat of terrorism, have forever changed our lives. **All** of our lives. Beyond the destruction of the World Trade Center twin towers and the tragic human toll that sad autumn day of 2001, our innocence also died that day. No longer were we safe on American soil; no longer were we safe if we were a civilian not fighting in our all-volunteer military; no longer were we safe if we weren't actively engaged in opposing the terrorists; no longer were we safe, even if we're just minding our own business. Since that day, we've learned that **any** American is vulnerable, no matter how innocent, disengaged or isolated they are from this fight.

"Any of us can die at any time, just because we're American. So you try to appreciate each good day."
—Giselle, 52, Administrator, Atlanta, GA

"It's like the Wild West. Violence is everywhere. And any of us can die at any time [from terrorism], no matter our station in life."
—Mario, 48, Transit Worker, New York City, NY

In fairness, we haven't all reacted uniformly to the barbaric 9/11 attacks. Some Americans pretend that the attacks never occurred, and have pretty much gone on living as if nothing has changed; still others have curtailed travel out of fear of another attack, and have taken a number of other actions to change their lifestyles. But these aren't the norms. Most Americans have responded to 9/11 in precisely the manner that most frustrates terrorists – by moving on with their lives, according to focus group respondents:

- **By continuing to travel**, domestically and throughout the world – though terror is always in the back of our minds, never far from consciousness.

While Americans travel, more than ever, **we do so while fully acknowledging the logistical and safety difficulties of travel**, as well as at least some of the dangers. We know we are going to face increased screening for travel, and the inconvenience of packing our liquids in separate plastic bags. In focus groups, people repeatedly tell us that they are mentally prepared for the rigors of travel –and think that travel is worth **all** the hassle post-9/11.

"It takes longer and it's more stressful to travel these days. But it's totally worth it."
—Annabelle, 38, Housewife, LaJolia, CA

"If traveling takes longer, takes more time, so be it. It's part of how I make my living, so I have to be prepared for it. Or at least tolerant of it."
—Hazel, 50, Domestic Help, Los Angeles, CA

Beyond travel, Americans are generally supportive of additional costs to keep our country safe, post-9/11. Airline surcharges and a larger budget deficit in Washington have caused barely a ripple, mostly because Americans understand the "new" costs of freedom. It's far less certain whether future costs will be met with the same smile and shrug of acceptance by American taxpayers.

"We all know that to stay safe will cost more – now and in the future. I mean, that goes without saying, really. And let's face it, most Americans feel this way."
—Arturo, 50, Restaurant Owner, Tustin, CA

"I'm not happy we have such a huge budget deficit. But that's just the way things are these days."
—Alex, 24, Teacher's Aide, Orland Park, IL

Safety Vs. Privacy – As we've already noted (and will again in a subsequent chapter), **most** Americans **are still very conflicted over the need for safety and security, versus the need for privacy**. Are we willing to accept X-ray machines that will literally undress us, if it keeps us safe? Do we care if someone knows what books we've take out of the library, if it helps keep us safe? It's just not clear at this stage, and won't be for quite some time. We will have to approach new issues relating to safety and security on a case-by-case basis.

The last and least tangible impact of the 9/11 attacks is "the psychological effect." I'm not a psychologist – and have never played one on TV – so it's challenging to explain this in quick order. But perhaps the best way to describe the "psychological" impact is to note that the 9/11 terrorist attack never quite leaves the back of our minds.

That is, we'll never quite forget the 9/11 attacks or their aftermath. And we'll always wonder if we could be next, much like the 3,000 unfortunate souls who perished that bright September day. So, while it hasn't impacted our interest in travel or most other aspects of our lives, it does cause **stress** – who hasn't left on a trip in the last six or seven years and wondered if it would be your last? So most of us are seemingly not impacted by terrorism, yet we'll never be able to forget, much less forgive.

'Til Death, Or Our Bank Accounts, Do Us Part — While terrorism has cast a large shadow over our lives, the changing face of **marriage** is a more home-grown change to our American lifestyles, and one worth noting.

We've observed very minor declines in the divorce rate in recent years, though about one out of every two marriages is still destined for failure.[22] However, we've also observed a very alarming trend in our focus groups, which we've subsequently explored in recent years

To be blunt, many current marriages, especially for Americans in their late twenties and early thirties, seem more a financial proposition than a love story. We don't mean to offend, dear readers, but we've sworn to be objective in profiling America for this book, and many marriages are still about love. But more and more marriages seem to be less about love and passion than about the need for financial security, or how many zeroes we have in our bank accounts. Over the past few decades, many American households have required two incomes, or two breadwinners, in order to maintain the standard of living they've come to expect. In talking to focus group respondents, they acknowledge that

---

[22] According to the U.S. Census Bureau, the divorce rate has actually dropped since 2002. At present, about 45% of all marriages end in divorce, down considerably from 50%+ in recent years

they are not as likely to have gotten married because they were deeply, passionately, head-over-heels in love. No, times have changed.

"As you get older, you just look for someone to hang with for the rest of your life."
—Ray, 42, Electrician, Columbus, OH

"Sure, financial stability counts a lot when deciding whether to get married. Maybe it's the most important thing."
—Dave, 50, Accountant, Highland Park, IL

"I'm sorry, but if you don't have a good job and a good future, I'm not marrying you, no matter how in love I am."
—Jorge, 50, Executive, Costa Mesa, CA

We've also learned from focus group respondents that it is just plain more difficult to meet people than in past decades. Many Americans are reluctantly single, not happily so.

"It is so hard to meet decent people, let me tell you."
—Cristy, 26, Office Worker, Pittsburgh, PA

"I'd love to get married, but where do you meet [other] people who want to get married, too? It just seems impossible these days."
—Estelle, 29, Executive, Hallandale, FL

Ultimately, the marriage quest is less about love for many Americans, than simply about finding somebody…anybody…to hang out with, in order to avoid dying alone. And what better way to evaluate potential mates than a thorough review of their finances…after all, if you're going to take the plunge, why not make sure that it's with someone financially solvent, if not downright affluent?

"I think it's perfectly okay to evaluate [a potential mate] based on their finances. It's just so important to living these days."
—Judith Anne, 30, Professional Dance Instructor, Colorado Springs, CO

"You bet I want to know all about a partner's finances. That's really important these days."
—Ingrid, 50, Business Owner, Cudahy, WI

Recall from our opening chapter that the American Dream has changed for many Americans – it's less about happiness and contentment in the house with the white picket fence than getting filthy, stinking rich.

I will confess that we are stumped in figuring out where this trend will ultimately lead. On the one hand, we could surmise that so many "loveless" marriages will ultimately lead to brisk action in divorce court. On the other hand, as long as two incomes are required to lead a comfortable life, perhaps these financial arrangements really are the way to go. Love is so serendipitous, crazy and unpredictable, but rate of return surely is not. Maybe this is the way marriage is **supposed** to go.

Whatever its impact on marriage, we believe that these "loveless" marriages are ultimately influencing our country in one major way – through declining birth rates.

"Who has the time or money to have kids anymore?"
—Phil, 36, Accountant, Akron, OH

"We just can't afford kids. Ever. It's really that simple."
—Dave, 50, CPA, Lincoln Park, IL

Married couples who are more determined to maximize their return on investment than a return to family values are less likely to have children. Kids are costly and impact careers in a major way. So while divorce rates may be dropping a bit, expect birth rates to plummet in coming years.

The Beatles once sang, "I don't care too much for money, money can't buy me love." Wow, if only they'd waited forty years or so.

But these aren't the only changes to our American lifestyle in recent years. No, we're just getting started…

Lord Of The Flies – Yes, I am probably dating myself to confess that we had to read *The Lord Of The Flies* when I was in high school. I was never quite sure why it was considered a "classic," but it was kind of, sort of, interesting, sort of. It's a story about a group of young boys shipwrecked on an island. Without adults, these kids must form their own society and develop a world built totally around pre-pubescent boys. Probably doesn't sound that interesting, after all.

But it does come to mind now, when I consider that we've now entered what I would term a "Lord Of The Flies" phase in American life. In simplest terms: kids rule. Oh, sure, unlike the book, we adults are still around, and we haven't elected a child as President, at least not yet.

No, our "Lord Of The Flies" phase is more about the exalted status that children occupy in American life. Our children obviously represent the future, a legacy to future generations. And for this reason, it's probably not a bad thing to make kids such a major priority in our country. But in focus groups, some people complain that children are, how shall we say...spoiled!

"Kids today think they can do anything...and they get away with it. Their parents are always there to bail 'em out, even when they're wrong."
—Olive, 46, Aerobics Instructor, San Jose, CA

"Kids today run roughshod over everybody. They act like there's no such thing as right and wrong."
—Maya, 54, Business Consultant, Longmont, CO

Okay, up to now, the evidence in favor of this lifestyle trend has been a bit soft. But take a closer look, and maybe there's something to it.

Every year, it seems, we hear how Americans **must** increase our spending on public education, before we relegate our kids to a lifetime of poverty and disgrace. Yet, according to Nicholas Jenny of The

Rockefeller Institute, inflation-adjusted, per-pupil spending on public education (K through 12) in the United States has increased by 12% over 1997 spending levels, and by nearly 15% since 1992. Our kids are anything but deprived.

If you haven't been to a Little League or youth soccer game in a while, by all means, head over. The kid without a trophy? Why, you won't find one. **Every** kid gets a trophy, because we don't want any child to ever feel what it's like to lose and be disappointed. (Never mind that some of these kids will soon live a lifetime of disappointment, and that we all experience defeat at some point.)

When I was a child, I always wanted to go to Disneyland or Disneyworld. I didn't care where – I just wanted a little Disney in my life. Alas, I didn't make it until adulthood. Somehow, though, I muddled through and was still able to piece together a decent life. But today's child is, um, different, apparently, as the following account, which originally ran in Tribune Media Services under the headline, "Disney Cruises Vacation Heaven For Kids," by Eileen Ogintz, notes:

(Tribune Media Services) – *It's well past the kids' bedtime, but no one is nagging the preschoolers and kindergartners to brush their teeth and go to sleep. Vacationers feed the stingrays on Castaway Cay, Disney's private island in the Bahamas.*

Instead, they're dressed to the nines (the girls, anyway) in full princess regalia before heading to a poolside pirate party, complete with fireworks, to get up close and personal with Goofy and all of his pirate friends aboard the Disney Wonder. Others are busy in the shipboard Oceaneer Club playing the latest video games, watching movies in seats designed to look like clam shells and climbing on the pirate ship play structure.

All of this is after they've seen a brand-new Broadway-style show – "Toy Story: The Musical," featuring all of their favorite characters from the popular film – and dined like royalty at dinner where the waiters not only knew their names but also performed magic tricks and were happy to get them anything they liked at no extra charge (a side of salmon with your chicken fingers...no problem!)

When my 5-year-old cousin Ethan Sitzman and his 3-year-old sister Hannah finally got back to their stateroom, they were thrilled that the steward, Pacifer Ticao, himself a young father from the Philippines, had fashioned a PJ Party with the kids' stuffed animals and a monkey he had made out of towels. The kids truly thought they'd arrived in vacation heaven.

And the list continues on...we don't spank kids because of the trauma this could induce...games like "Red Rover" have been eliminated at lunch time school yards because they punish children for losing...family sections are set aside at restaurants, so that some children can limber up their arms while they throw food across the room...some schools no longer give traditional "A through F" grades to young students, for fear that this will cause self-esteem problems in underperforming students...and we certainly could never spank children – look what happened to my generation of spankees. (What **did** happen to us? Ummm...)

So maybe we **have** lost perspective with children in America. Every time I think that perhaps that could be an exaggeration, I remember Thanksgiving when I was a child. We had seven children in my family, so when Grandma and Grandpa came to town, myself and two brothers – the youngest of our brood – were relegated to a card table in the corner. Our goal during the two-week holiday visit was to be neither seen nor heard by adults during meals, for this was my parent's time, and my grandparent's time. After all, the rest of the year was for us.

Thirty years later, it was customary for my nieces and nephews – you know, today's kids – to occupy prime real estate at the holiday dinner table. Often, the entire meal hinged on when they wanted to eat, what they wanted to eat, what they wanted to talk about. You get the picture.

When I suggested to one sibling that a nice card table for kids might be in order at future meals, she responded in the only way she could. "Are you crazy?" she screamed. "We don't want to make the kids feel bad. It might give them a complex." Indeed.

Take This Job And... – As we noted in the opening chapter to the book, Americans are absolutely infatuated with the idea of retiring early. Of course, wanting not to work anymore probably has a lot to do with that.

But beyond the tedious nature of our day-to-day jobs, what we've also found in our focus group work is that retiring early has become a **major** goal for many Americans. In other words, we're driven as much by the goal – the actual date of retirement – as anything else.

"I've set a goal of retiring exactly five years before the regularly scheduled teacher retirement date for my age."
—Gustav, 48, Retired, Tacoma,

"It's important for me to retire early. It will show how prosperous I've become and how much I've achieved. So, yeah, it's important to me."
—Katherine, 31, Housewife, Gardenia, CA

So there may be a lot of Americans hitting the early bird special at Denny's for dinner at some point in the future, what with all these retirements. Some day, we may even see college grads retire **before** they graduate and get their first job.

On a serious note, this early retirement binge will further pressure our already thin labor force. We can only hope that productivity rises along with early retirement. Regardless, some day soon the office of the future may look mighty empty.

Over there! Over there!... – Anywhere, but over here. Americans in the early 2000's have been overcome by a rising tide of **internationalism.** From travel to food, fashion and even TV programming, Americans of all ages and socio-economic groups are most interested in what's going on overseas or at least beyond our borders.

> *"You have to pay attention to what goes on outside the U.S."*
> —Toni, 28, Chef, Rapid City, SD

> *"I learn a lot by watching other countries."*
> —Ziggy, 40, Unemployed, Bronx, NY

Based on the focus groups, we're not sure that this trend represents anything more than idle curiosity or boredom with the sameness of American life, rather than an outright rejection of America.

> *"I just get tired of the same food all the time, so I've sort of learned to experiment with international cuisine. It's fun."*
> —Smitty, 30, Teacher, Owings Mills, MD

> *"I like to see some of the shows that are popular in Europe. You never know, they might have better [TV shows] than ours."*
> —Danielle, 28, Housewife, Santa Fe, NM

However, we'd be remiss not to report that part of this trend does including the emerging need for Americans to seek approval from foreign countries and international citizens, for everything from our foreign policy to the food we eat. A generation ago, Americans took pride in our world standing – the biggest economy, the best Army, and the highest standard of living, to name but a few components of this standing. At times, we were almost drunk with power. But times clearly have changed – we seem more concerned with what the rest of the world thinks of us, than with our actual standing in the world', or what we've actually achieved.

> *"I don't think anyone in the world likes us anymore."*
> —Annie, 38, Substitute Teacher

> *"The whole world is pretty mad at us for the Iraq war, don't you think?"*
> —Ismael, 49, Laborer, Anaheim, CA

We see an emerging trend in all of this – what we've termed "American Guilt." Part of the international community's presumed criticism and disapproval of America is that we often feel guilty about our country and its resources, even without criticism. It's a reflexive reaction. If we Americans excel, achieve, or just plain have an abundance of something, then some of us feel guilty.

American Guilt

What do Americans feel guilty about?

☆ Our energy consumption.

☆ American food supplies.

☆ Our carbon "footprint."

☆ Our military power.

☆ The freedoms enjoyed by Americans day-to-day.

☆ America's natural resources.

☆ Children's health.

☆ American wastefulness.

☆ Our overall consumption of goods and services.

There are two (potentially) serious consequences to American Guilt. First, we may not achieve our full potential in some areas if we cave in to feelings of guilt. At some point in the future, it's likely that Americans will legislate curbs on our carbon footprint, or greenhouse gas emissions. Imagine the damage to our economy if global warming isn't quite the problem some believe. (This issue is discussed in more depth in the next chapter.)

The other consequence is that we may not act (forcefully or quickly) in some cases, given our serious loss of perspective. The notion that Americans are loathed worldwide? Hogwash, as those of you who travel internationally will attest. Sure, some people don't like us. But most international citizens still have a great deal of respect for the American way of life. But imagine if we fail to lead an international coalition of some sort – say, against Iran's nuclear weapons – because we feel that the U.S. no longer can exert any moral leadership, given how we're loathed worldwide. That would be a tragic mistake, for us and the world.

There are a few more lifestyle trends to note before we head to other aspects of American life, and they're summarized in the remainder of this chapter.

I Worship Thee, Al Gore - We don't really worship Al Gore and the environmental movement, do we?

At first glance, you might think this is one of the most sweeping or radical changes in our American lifestyle, to date. But it's really not. Right now, it's more smoke than fire, more mirrors than magic tricks. In short, we really haven't changed our habits regarding the environment in the United States, at least not yet.

Oh, we huff and puff and flap our gums on the environment...

"We gotta save them polar bears."
—Terrence, 50, Lawyer, Roswell, NM

"I didn't know the polar bears were in trouble. Why do we have to save them?"
—Alvin, 58, City Worker, Birmingham, AL

When it comes to the environment, we're mostly talk right now, even with gas at $4 to $5 per gallon. We talk about buying hybrid cars, but we don't. We'd all like to see solar cells on our roofs, so that we'd be net contributors of energy, not consumers, but we don't want to spend the money. We'd like thousands of wind turbines, but we know they aren't very reliable. And we all talk about biking to work, but very few of us actually do – it might mess up our hair! In short, we're mostly talk when it comes to the environment.

Our focus groups indicate that most of us recycle, and we're also beginning to drive less as a conservation effort. Given the intense rhetoric from Americans about the environment, we expect lifestyle patterns to change significantly in the near future, at least with respect to the environment.

*"I would ride my bike to wo*rk more to save money and gas, but I'd look like hell when I got there."
—Addie, 56, Account Executive, Urbandale, IA

But a word of caution. While most Americans do consider the environment a crucial issue, certainly critical to the future, it's not at all clear how much we're willing to sacrifice – if anything – to boost the environment. Traditionally, Americans value their finances over the environment, and we expect them to do so in the future.

Changes in our environmental lifestyle are more likely when bolstered by economics. In other words, when solar panels are $400 to install, not $40,000, Americans will be far more likely to change. In the meantime, it's more rhetoric than action. (The environmental movement will be discussed again in the next chapter.)

Adios, er, Farewell, Miss Manners – One aspect of modern American life which we shouldn't be particularly proud of is our rude, crude society. We Americans have, on balance, become downright nasty in recent years. From poor manners to our crude use of language, we just plain seem uncivil at times. However, we'll wait a bit to plunge in-depth into this section, as we have an entire chapter devoted to this titled, appropriately, *The Rise of the [Jerry] Springer Generation*. In the meantime, if you've ever been overseas and immediately been pegged an American, don't feel bad. It's a reputation we've richly earned.

A Collection Of Collectors – Once upon a time, the American pastime was said to have been baseball. Now, we are a nation of collectors. Maybe it hasn't risen yet to the level of national pastime, but it's not far off. In fact, collecting, in general, has probably become the top leisure-time pursuit for Americans, other than watching TV.

> *"Doesn't everybody collect these days."*
> —Sam, 22, Student, Norman, OK

> *"If you aren't collecting something, it's probably because you're dead."*
> —Abe, 30, Professional Collector, Manhattan, NY

Every focus group we do is a bit like a United Nations gathering of collectors. Stamps, coins and baseball cards are usually represented, with many groups containing a Barbie Doll collector, as well. But what makes America truly unique are the non-traditional collectors:

COLLECTIONS WE'VE HEARD ABOUT IN FOCUS GROUPS

Dead Lizard Skins

Dead Baseball Players (Cards; not their Bodies)

Bank Debit Cards

Custom License Plates

McDonald's Toy Giveaways

Gay Superheroes

Women's High Heels (But Not The Shoes)

Passport Stamps (From Different Countries)

$1,000 Chips From Casinos

International Butterflies (As Opposed To Domestic U.S.)

The Inner Core Of Old Softballs

And this list only scratches the surface of collections we've heard about in focus groups. Americans are nothing if not creative and passionate about collecting – and often, we pour significant amounts of money into our hobbies.

With the invention of eBay and our focus on materialism (remember Chapter 1), you can hardly seem to go wrong collecting. There is practically a market for anything, as the *Antiques Roadshow* (on

PBS) or *The Incurable Collector* (on A & E) or any of the other shows on antiques and collectibles will attest.

We're not sure if the collecting bug is a virus, or is somehow programmed into our DNA in the States, but the bug has bitten us hard. Think for a moment about all the collections you're aware of, just in your household. We thought so.

And if you don't have a collection yet, remember the words of an ancient collector in one of our focus groups, to one of his non-collecting brethren:

> *"Never throw anything away. Sooner or later, you'll find*
> *something to collect."*
> —Robles, 30, Limousine Driver, Miami, FL

And to think that Mom insisted I throw the garbage out once a week when I was in high school. Oh, my misspent youth!

Hooray For Hollywood – We couldn't end this discussion of changes in the American lifestyle without discussing one of our biggest leisure time pursuits, which is anything related to Hollywood stars and famous people. That's right. America is not only the home of the free and the brave, but also the home of stargazers…and we aren't talking about astronomy.

From our focus group work, it's become abundantly clear that we're in love with celebrity in this country, particularly Hollywood celebrities. Doubtless, you're wondering why this is considered a changing pattern in our American lifestyles – haven't we always been fascinated by Hollywood?

> *"I just love, love, love, Hollywood gossip."*
> —Tara, 28, Sales Representative, Carmel, CA

> *"Like anyone else, I am interested in what the stars do."*
> —Carl, 38, Plumber, Stamford, CT

The answer is a resounding "no." Sure, we've always been somewhat curious about Hollywood stars, rock musicians and the like. Recall the fan magazines of the 1950's and 1960's, how our lives seemed to hinge on Rock Hudson's newest girlfriend, or where the Beatles liked to stay in New York.

What's changed is that we not only appreciate the work of these stars – movies, TV shows, records and such – but we now want to know **every** detail about their lives, from whether they had teeth extracted to who they've voted for in the last four Presidential elections. (Don't laugh – I seriously read an article once on that very subject about a current star.) In other words, our fandom has turned into full-fledged mania in many respects.

For this reason, we read about their sex lives, tour their second homes, bedroom by bedroom, and find out how much they tip when dining in Times Square after a turn on Broadway. We have our traditional "tabloid" magazines like *The Star* and *The National Enquirer* – plus new magazines like *OK* and *In Style* have popped up, due to our insatiable curiosity about the stars. We still have *Entertainment Tonight* and *Access Hollywood* on the tube, but also a new spate of gossip shows on E! and syndicated shows like *TMZ*, founded by the intrepid Harvey Levin. Where else can you watch cameras chase a tipsy Lindsay Lohan from a nightclub to her car, or enjoy watching paparazzi trample each other while keeping a vigil outside Angelina Jolie's maternity ward in Nice? And don't forget all the drivel on the Internet.

On the face of it, there isn't really anything wrong with our devotion to the stars and their lives…but beneath the surface, it's become a somewhat unhealthy obsession. Do we really need to know so much about these people? Perhaps a better question is **why** do we need to know so much?

But the truly dangerous aspect to this obsession with stardom is that many Americans not only look to these entertainers for harmless fun and amusement, but also as role models to be followed and, ultimately, copied. We used to mimic their fashion sense…now, seventeen girls from Gloucester High in Massachusetts have become pregnant, in homage to all the Hollywood stars and pop stars who've become pregnant recently – from Angelina Jolie to Gwen Stefani and Jamie Lynn Spears. Never mind that teen pregnancy in working class America is most definitely a different life than pregnancy among pop stars and Hollywood divas.

Beyond our strange obsession with the personal lives of stars, we also want to know about the political beliefs of the stars, from who they're going to vote for, and why, to their stand on the issues. But the question running through many of our minds is…why? Some stars are unquestionably bright and well versed on specific issues, while others are as dim as the burned out bulbs on the Statue Of Liberty. Either way, why do we care about the political and social beliefs of someone, merely because they're a star? It's roughly akin to asking a politician some question about the lighting and costumes in a recent blockbuster movie. (Think about it.)

We can only hope that our fascination with stardom ends soon. Or that we start pondering the wisdom of the glitterati. During the long-ago Presidential election of 2004, Alec Baldwin promised to vacate the country if George Bush was re-elected. As one of our focus group respondents wryly noted…

"I'll be happy to pitch in with his move. Just tell me when and where, and I'll be there."
—Alex, 43, Laborer, Danbury, CT

The Future

How will the American lifestyle change in the future? Why, if you knew that, you would be rich beyond belief. Americans are a dynamic, effervescent people who aren't living in a test tube, but in the real world. In other words, our world is very complex and combustible. And where that takes us down the road is anybody's guess.

We often play word association games, especially early in focus groups, in order to build interest in our topic and establish a context for understanding the comments. In one group in Orlando several years ago, we asked the respondents to write down a word or a phrase to describe the American lifestyle – you know, all the things we've been discussing the past two chapters. When we asked the group to share their answers out loud, an older woman with an accent of some sort in the back of the room, silent up to that point, suddenly jumped forward in her seat to share her answer.

"American" she nearly shouted, before lapsing into a Cheshire-cat smile. Then, as if to make sure that no one had missed her answer, she shouted "American" again.

And who could argue with that? Our lifestyle is, at its most basic, American. Very American, at that.

Chapter 7:

New Deal? Try Raw Deal

☆ ☆ ☆ ☆ ☆

"In general, the art of government consists in taking as much money as possible from one party of citizens to give to the other."
—Voltaire

"Life under a good government is rarely dramatic; life under a bad government is always so."
—Oscar Wilde

"I gotta figure out what each guy is offering to me, you know, as a voter. In other words, I gotta add it all up. Once I figure that out, I can tell you who I'll be voting for. It's all about what I get out of the deal."
—Lennie, 52, Truck Driver, Flushing, NY

We begin this chapter with yet another quiz – I simply can't resist!

Imagine for a moment that a survey has been conducted for your business, and it finds that **less than 10% of all your customers think you're doing a good job**. That's right – less than one out of every ten customers is really happy with your company. Now, knowing what you know about business, do you consider this number to be…

❏   Good?

❏   Bad?

❏   Just Plain Terrible?

Okay, go ahead and deliberate on this one, if you must. Oh, and by the way, you might want to know that this one isn't hypothetical. There really **is** an organization that has less than 10% of its customers satisfied with its performance. The organization? Why, that would be the U.S. Congress, in public opinion polls taken during the Summer of 2008. Oh, and the customers? Why, that's us, the citizens of the United States – remember, we are **voters** and **taxpayers**, too. Guess you're not enjoying this quiz much anymore, are you?

I have a confession to make to you, dear readers. When we were originally outlining this book, there wasn't any room for, or interest in, including a chapter on government, politics and the like. After all, we reasoned, there are literally hundreds, if not thousands, of books on politics released each year. And if you start talking politics, that has a tendency to change the nature of the book and its related dialogue. To be clear, with today's heightened level of partisanship, a chapter on government and politics can be poison to the tone of the book.

However, the outline for the book changed – and markedly at that – while actually writing this book, especially after completing the two preceding chapters on lifestyle. The reasoning was, ultimately, quite simple. Even though more than 300 million people are proud to call themselves Americans, the government continues to exert a major influence on **each** of our lives, whether we realize it, or not.

Ultimately, that's the threshold for inclusion in this book. If something influences our lives in a **major fashion**, and is something that our focus group respondents have discussed and provided insight on, then it's included in this book. It has to be, since *America In Focus* is ultimately a book which profiles Americans during this first decade of the new Millennium.

So the ensuing chapter will spend very little time on traditional partisan politics – we (myself and my Editors) decided that is for other authors to cover, some other day (especially authors who have actual expertise or experience with politics). Rather, this chapter is about how government has become such a major part of our lives. Specifically, we want to focus on a variety of **emerging trends** in government and politics which have conspired to thrust government into the forefront of our lives.

The Raw(est?) Deal

Younger readers – or maybe those under the age of 100 – may not be able to remember when Presidential terms earned unique monikers. But they did. Teddy Roosevelt, early in the 20th Century, presided over the **Square Deal**; his cousin, FDR, was President during a time of profound change, aptly named the **New Deal**, which was then followed by Harry Truman's **Fair Deal**, a bad marketing idea if ever there was one – i.e., only a "fair" deal? Ultimately, JFK's **New Frontier** wrapped up this era. (Apparently, Republican Presidents like Ike, Nixon and Ford refused to participate!) However, it's not really clear why these colorful names, and epochs in American politics, ultimately died out, but…

…It's clearly time to reintroduce this tradition to Americans, if for no other reason than it seems like such a fun, nostalgic concept. So if we stop and think about **this** era, it's clearly marked by:

- A **profound** dislike of government, overall.
- Strong dislike with what the government does for (or provides to) each of us, much less what it achieves on our behalf.
- Tremendous **distrust** of government; we don't feel like the government is on **our** side any more. It's on its own side.

So what shall we call this era in American politics and government? Why, uh, this, er, couldn't be anything but, just has to be…drumroll please…the **Raw Deal**. And when you think about it, who isn't getting a raw deal from the government these days?

> *"The government just screws us at every turn. It's just one big raw deal, when you get down to it."*
> —Kate, 52, Physician, Lehigh Valley, PA

> *"Man, you look at our taxes. What a raw deal."*
> —Jon, 46, Police Officer, Philadelphia, PA

> *"The government is just one raw deal, for all of us, right now."*
> —Billie, 46, Hygienist, Spokane, WA

It's clear that we can't take credit for this name. No, the credit goes to the tens of thousands of people interviewed over the years in our focus groups – these are but a sampling of the "raw deal" quotes in our files. We tip our hats to you, focus group participants, as the Raw Deal fits this era like a proverbial glove.

So what is the Raw Deal? As promised, we will be taking a look at emerging trends in government and politics which, not so coincidentally, are the philosophical underpinnings of the Raw Deal. Is this truly a Raw Deal? More raw than we can ever imagine.

Ask What Your Country Can Do For YOU!

Before we can really understand the Raw Deal, it's first necessary to assess our expectations for government. After all, these expectations not only shape our government and directly impact what we expect from government, but they also have much to do with our satisfaction with government.

Almost fifty years ago, President John F. Kennedy sounded a call to action that is memorable, even today. During his Inaugural Address, Kennedy implored that we should, "Ask not what your country can do for you. Ask what you can do for your country."

Kennedy's meaning was clear – it is up to each one of us to serve this great country in some way.

Based upon what we hear in focus groups, Kennedy's philosophy could not be any further from how we actually feel today.

> *"The government don't do nothing good for my family now."*
> —Saul, 60, Disabled, Yonkers, NY

> *"I want to ask everyone…what have you gotten out of this government lately? The answer is, 'Not much.'"*
> —Harding, 40, Business Owner, Fort Wayne, IN

Clearly, it's not about what we can do for the country – no, the government's role is to give something, anything, to **us**, as **often as possible** – a tax refund, welfare, grants, public education, financial aid for college, insurance for our home destroyed in a tornado or hurricane, inoculation against a new disease, disaster relief, a tax break, flood insurance – if the government is offering, then we're taking, or at least accepting. And that's really the essence of the Raw Deal. It's about what the government can – but mostly should – do for us, now and in the future.

How and why has our attitude on the role of government shifted over time? In truth, we're not sure that it has. After all, Kennedy's soaring rhetoric was really designed to affect a major change in our attitude and outlook toward government – perhaps that's why it is so memorable, even today.

But regardless of whether our selfish outlook toward government represents true change, or not, it is influencing our opinion of government in a major way. The more we expect from government, the less it seems to deliver. It's simply part of the expectations game. The more we expect, the harder it is to perform – it's really that simple.

So as we ponder our changing relationship with government, it's wise to remember our expectations. For in the end, it's these expectations which are most strongly influencing government's role in American society.

The "Know Nothing" Era

Okay, I admit that there really isn't a nice way to say this, so here goes. Americans are woefully **uninformed** about our government and politics; some might even say we're downright dumb when it comes to government and politics. But that sure doesn't stop us from having opinions, or spouting them to anyone who will listen. (Yes, dear readers, the following quotes, regrettably, are real!)

"Who's the President, again?"
—Donnie, 30, Sanitation Worker, Towson, MD

"If Bush dies, who takes over? Is it like the King of England, where it will be his brother or mother taking over?"
—Kirkland, 42, Electrician, Lake Elsinore, CA

"As soon as I figure out how many Senators there are for this state, I might call one of them to complain."
—Andie, 40, Housewife, Algiers, LA

"If Bush loses the election, do they put him to death?"
—Eddie Ray, 28, Laborer, Jackson, MS

"Our capital is in Washington, right? Seattle, Washington?"
—John, 23, Student, Pullman, WA

In focus groups, we've found that Americans aren't just ignorant of the small minutiae that sometimes passes for government – no, they are uninformed about nearly everything relating to politics and government.

"Who's that secretary of state chick again? What's her name?"
—Del, 30, Unemployed, Manchester, MO

"I can't remember who we fought in Vietnam, but I know we beat them, right?"
—Ang Sahn, 31, Chemist, San Francisco, CA

The only exception that we've run across in the last decade to our "know nothing" Americans in focus groups is a group that we've come to call the "politically active" – or PA's for short. PA's are typically current or former candidates, financial donors to campaigns, close relatives of candidates and locally engaged politicians (ward captains, aldermen and such). PA's are usually as knowledgeable as possible, and put to shame the majority "know nothings."

Alas, we remain a country largely composed of "know nothings" – citizens who know next to nothing about politics and government, or who know enough to be dangerous – i.e., they know a little bit, but not enough to make informed decisions.

And that's the rub. We Americans, on balance, aren't a little bit dumb about politics. No, we are **woefully** uninformed, and not just about the number of Senators in each state, or whether our country's capitol building lines the banks of the Puget Sound in Seattle. No, we are ignorant on any number of public policy fronts:

"Isn't inflation a real problem?"
—Mark, 36, Actor/Waiter, Studio City, CA

Note: It hadn't been from 1982 to at least the Summer of 2008 – though it's something we hear about routinely in focus groups, not just in the single quote above (from 2001).

"What if Iran attacks us with nuclear weapons?"
—Stacey, 37, Consultant, Chantilly, VA

Note: Through 2008 and the foreseeable future, Iran does not possess a missile capable of reaching the U.S., except perhaps on a cruise liner. (Does this make it a cruise missile, I wonder?)

> *"You know that Judge on the Supreme Court, Judge Wapner?"*
> —Eta, 58, Housewife, Great Falls, MT

Note: Venerable Judge Joseph Wapner was the original judge on the ***People's Court*** TV show; alas, despite this experience, he was never appointed to the Supreme Court.

In defense of America's seeming ignorance regarding politics and government, we are a terribly busy people these days. That is, there is a reason why we have the world's biggest economy, the best military in the world, and the most affluent society in the world – we work hard! So in a sense, it's not surprising that we aren't exactly knowledgeable when it comes to matters of government and current events. Who has the time?

> *"I am so busy these days that I don't have time even to read a newspaper!"*
> —Maxine, 32, Elementary School Teacher, Palo Alto, CA

> *"Current events? The only current event in my world is my life."*
> —Curly, 40, Office Worker, Sugarland, TX

Unfortunately, busyness alone probably doesn't exempt us from the need for some basic level of knowledge about government and politics. The reason is that an uninformed citizenry often makes just plain bad decisions as voters and citizens. We aren't sure who our friends are throughout the world – e.g., is Pakistan one of the good guys, or not? We don't fully understand the energy "crisis" which has gripped our country (in varying degrees) since the early 1970's – is nuclear power safe? Should we drill offshore for oil, even in Alaska? Is a budget deficit okay? Or how big of a deficit? Would we be better off raising taxes?

At several points throughout this book, we've referenced that a specific subject could turn out to be the whole book, or a whole **other** book. And that's certainly true here. We could probably spend a whole separate book discussing public policy dilemmas facing the U.S. Alas, we have more material to cover. But I still wish that we Americans were better informed about matters relating to politics and government. I'm not sure about you, but I'd probably sleep better at night if we were.

The Amazing President

The Amazing President could be a comic book title, a new video game, or even a carnival side-show act at the little carnival that parks for a week in your town each year. Unfortunately, though, it's none of those. Instead, it's the derisive term I've come to use to describe many Americans' attitude toward our American President, another factor that is having a significant impact on our outlook for government.

> *"I blame President Bush for everything that has gone wrong. Everything."*
> —Emily, 24, Student, Englewood, CO

> *"What is the President going to do to help us?"*
> —Francis, 36, Education, Cincinnati, OH

Specifically, The Amazing President refers to the expectations that many Americans now have for our President – he is now thought by many to be a superman-like creature who is responsible for **everything** from local pet control policies to thermo-nuclear war, or the fate of mankind. It's quite a range of job skills that we expect for our Amazing President.

"I hold the President responsible, local or national. Absolutely."
—Jean, 62, Housewife, Farmington, MI

Our focus groups in recent years have detected a **distinct change** in how Americans view the Presidency. Focus group respondents now hold the President responsible for virtually anything and everything, even nature itself. Hurricane blow your house down? Blame the President. Family member gunned down by homicidal maniac with a gun? Call the President – it must be his crime bill. Family finances shrinking since your primary wage earner was laid off? Maybe the President can spot you a few bucks or get you a job! Test scores at the local junior high decline? Why, you know who to call – and who to blame. And we're not kidding – this particular list of tasks for our President has actually been mentioned in our focus groups.

Americans now tend to think of their President as a glorified Mayor, responsible for **everything** in our lives, from our safety to our pocketbooks. Whenever anything goes wrong – be it Hurricane Katrina or a lost Social Security check – blame the Prez!

"I sure wish the President would fly down to take a look at the areas hit by the tornado last spring."
—Elton, 42, Business Owner, Altamonte Springs, FL

"I wish President Bush could see all the people who are unemployed in this county. I mean, really see them."
—Becky, 33, Unemployed, Virginia Beach, VA

"The President has lost us that war in Iraq."
—Mark, 40, Fitness Instructor, El Segundo, CA

Part of this phenomenon is that the President has become the repository for many of our hopes and dreams in life – a symbol, if you will. Some Americans have an unhealthy obsession with the holder of this high office, though most will never come close to meeting the

President, much less having any sort of relationship with him or her. Regardless, when life deals us a setback, we Americans now tend to blame the President.

> *"My economy's not so good. I blame the President for that."*
> —Jill, 28, Radio Personality, Mauston, WI

> *"You have to hold the guy at the top responsible. Absolutely. And that's the President. So when things go wrong, I blame him."*
> —Don, 40, Physical Education Teacher, Golden, CO

And the unhealthy part of this Presidential obsession? Well in many, or most, cases, the President has little or nothing to do with our lives, regardless of the outcome or circumstances. From economic fortunes to our personal happiness, it's mostly up to us, and not the President.

I know what you're probably thinking right here – perhaps it's President Bush, specifically, and not the Presidency, in general, which we now hold responsible for everything under the sun. In other words, this could be another way for Americans to manifest their dislike for the current (as the book was being written) occupant of the White House. With apologies to Bush backers and hackers alike, the President's approval ratings **are** at an all-time low based on polling; the dislike of our current President is real and palpable.

However, our focus groups have indicated over time that the trend toward viewing our President as a Glorified World Mayor started long before George W. Bush, with suggestions of this trend while Clinton and Bush the Elder occupied the White House. In other words, this does appear to be part of a larger, longer term trend, unrelated to political parties or specific White House occupants.

> *"I hold Clinton responsible for our local economy, for sure."*
> —Ashlie, 23, Teacher, Charlotte, NC (January, 1998)

"Bush [the Elder] should care about what goes on here locally."
—Phil, 51, Office Worker, E. Hartford, CT (August, 1991)

There appears to be something else at work here. Specifically, we believe that Americans pinning all their hopes and dreams on the President, and the torrent of criticism for the President when anything goes wrong, is related to that first trend we identified in this chapter – namely, our lack of knowledge about government. Please follow along as we explain.

Most Americans in our focus groups know who our President is; in fact, many more than know our Secretary of State, or even about arcane legislative matters before the Congress. So, as we become less and less knowledgeable about the intricacies of government, the President – regardless of party or background – becomes the symbol for our hopes, dreams, fears and even our dissatisfaction. In effect, in this complicated age, the President has become the (lone) face of government. He is a convenient target for our hope, but also for our contempt should anything go wrong. He **is** the government, according to many Americans.

"The President is ultimately responsible for everything that goes on in government. Everything."
—Percy, 61, Musician, Chicago, IL

"You're damn right I hold him [the President} responsible when something goes wrong here [in his local home town]. He's at the top."
—Elsa, 56, Insurance Adjuster, Haddonfield, NJ

And why are we taking time to discuss this now? Well, it's worth noting that most future Presidents are likely to be terribly unpopular, on the whole. In simplest terms, it's likely that no man or woman is up to the job of being responsible for **everything** in our lives.

In other words, as long as we hold the President responsible for so much, it's highly unlikely that anyone can live up to the job. (Yes, President Clinton's popularity ratings at the conclusion of his term do fly in the face of this; however, his popularity ratings since he left office fall more in line with this.) The Presidency has often been described as the most difficult job in the world – but, given the range of issues on which Americans now hold the President responsible, the job difficulty has been increased two- or threefold.

The other reason for noting this trend is more pragmatic – you know, elections and things. We believe that the Presidency is moving toward an era of more **one-term Presidencies**, much like the last few decades of the 19th Century. Traditionally, most Presidents are elected to two terms (winning re-election) – but not in the future. As long as Americans hold the President responsible for such an impossibly diverse list of public policy issues, it will be difficult for any President to achieve the goals of a majority of Americans – or to keep people voting for them. Reagan, Clinton and Bush (The Younger) have all been two-term Presidents since 1980 – they may be the last for a while.

Terror, Terror, Go Away!

It's unclear how historians might ultimately view the War on Terror. Typically, it takes ten, twenty or more years before historians can adequately view the context and impact of people and events, and help place them in perspective for posterity's sake. Regardless, it is clear that the War on Terror is the single most critical issue facing this country right now, and that it is having a tangible impact on our views of government.

The importance of the War on Terror cannot be understated, as it's literally a "life or death" issue. We sometimes forget that a significant portion of the world would enjoy watching the United States collapse. That's right, they'd love to see our democratic form of government stamped out – and with it, the tremendous affluence that Americans have enjoyed for most of our country's history.

However, discussing the geopolitical origins of the War on Terror is not the point of this book – and so we will exit this subject in an expeditious manner.

However, we can't fully ignore that the War on Terror is having a major impact on our relations and views on our government. For starters, it's had a major impact on our last few elections, according to our focus group respondents:

> *"I think [President George W.] Bush is better able to take on the terrorists. That's why I voted for him."*
> —Claudia, 47, Consultant, Pittsburgh, PA

> *"No question, I am going to vote for the candidate who's better able to manage the terrorism issue – now and in the future.*
> —Arnie, 58, Business Owner, Mequon, WI

And it's likely to continue having a major impact on our political outcomes for the foreseeable future. Life and death issues are simply that important.

Beyond electoral outcomes, several other tangible impacts of the War on Terror are likely to occur in the future:

- We will continue debating safety and security versus the need for privacy and human rights for years to come. In order to fight the bad guys, it is sometimes necessary to give away our rights and/or our privacy. On the other hand, how far will we go to remain safe? That is the crux of the debate, and why it may take a while to solve.

- All future leaders – from elected officials to appointees and Cabinet members will be evaluated in the context of their terror-fighting credentials.

- At some point, we'll need to decide whether this War on Terror is a real war, requiring significant resources to fight, or a symbolic war. This point, and our country's ultimate decision, draw ever closer, the longer we go without being attacked.

"We need to fight the War on Terror, every day and in every way."
—Celeste, 33, Model, Los Angeles, CA

"This so-called war is a sham. It's time to forget about it and move on."
—Beth, 26, Administrative Assistant, Sacramento, CA

Al Gore – Hero Or Charlatan?

A potentially bigger threat to many of us isn't the terrorists themselves, but the rise of the eco-terrorists. Who, you're wondering? You know, the **eco-terrorists.**

Eco-terrorists are often opportunists – including some just plain bad people – who are looking to dominate our lives and coerce specific behaviors under the guise of being concerned about the environment. They threaten everything from the way we make a living to our freedom to travel, recreate, and live our lives as we have for generations, freedoms and all.

Once you stop and think about it, it isn't terribly difficult to spot eco-terrorists in your individual life. Recognize any of the following?

- Has your City Council passed a law banning plastic bags in grocery stores – even if you bring your own? Or are they charging you if you don't bring your own bag to the store?

- Have any earnest school administrators banned specific substances from your child's back-to-school lists because they are no longer eco-friendly?

- Are you encouraged, or required, to ride a bike or carpool to work on certain days?

- Has one of your favorite fast-food restaurants changed the packaging on your food, supposedly because it's more recyclable?

Okay, okay – maybe the aforementioned list of "eco-terrorist" activities doesn't cause you to lose sleep, or to lose even one drop of sweat. But just wait – these are only the first few eco-terrorist attacks. Soon, eco-terrorists of all stripes will try to seize even more of your freedoms, such as:

- What you can – and can't – use to build your house.

- What you can set your house's thermostat at – have a cold? Forget it, you'll be told how warm you can be on those brisk winter days in an effort to "save" energy.

- What foods are grown – and how they're grown.

- How often you can water your lawn – if you live in a community that still allows lawns.

- When you go to work – which days, and for how many hours.

- Whether you can take a summer vacation with the family via a jet.

- Being required by your Homeowners Association to purchase specific appliances, based on energy ratings.

- Being charged for each bag of garbage you generate.

And this list is just a start. There will be many more infringements on our freedoms in the near future.

It is true that not every item on our new eco-regulations list is terribly onerous or demands significant personal sacrifice. And it's also true that not every eco-terrorist is a self-centered control freak who's out to rob us of personal freedoms.

But that's what makes this issue so interesting going forward. Theoretically, nearly **every** American is pro-environment. Don't kid yourself – they really are. We've almost never run across someone in a focus group who's willing to admit to being anti-environment. This is as close as we've come:

"I guess I can say I'm in favor of the environment, if you put a gun to my head."
—Stacia, 58, Housewife, Baltimore, MD

"I don't personally recycle. But I'm in favor of it. I'm just too lazy to do it myself."
—Errol, 34, Executive, Appleton, WI

In the future, we'll **all** be asked to change how we live and asked to pass judgment on many new ideas – all under the guise of preserving the environment. Further, we'll sometimes be asked to make these sacrifices while fatcats or hypocritical politicians don't sacrifice at all. Want to lower your thermostat while John Edwards heats his thirty thousand square foot mansion without similar restrictions? Didn't think so.

In the end, all I can advise you is to be very wary of the eco-terrorists. Always ask yourself whether you are willing to trade freedom for the promised eco-impact. It seems a question that will always be worth considering. Always.

Yikes, It's The Taxman!

Unlike that great Beatles song of the past, few of us regard the mythical taxman with anything but contempt. The Internal Revenue Service conjures negative, horrific images to most adult Americans, to the point where an entire industry offering tax relief has sprung up. (You've undoubtedly seen the commercials with stern-faced pitchmen offering to help **you** beat the IRS for just pennies on the dollar.)

But even more frightening, at least to some Americans, is this country's aw-shucks attitude toward taxes these days. Consequently, they are going up, up, up before our very eyes.

First, a bit of history. It may surprise some Americans to learn that the income tax wasn't even created until the 20th Century, much less the good ol' IRS.

"I think the Constitution mentions that we all have to pay income taxes."
—Amy, 33, Consultant, Washington, D.C.

"It's part of citizenship and the Constitution that we support the government through taxes."
—Eric, 33, Engineer, Philadelphia, PA

Wrong-o. Before the invention of the income tax, the only taxes typically collected were duties on international trade – you remember all that stuff about tariffs that we learned in history class? And contrary to popular belief, there is nothing in the Constitution about income taxes and the IRS. Those are manmade inventions.

From jokes on the old Bob Hope TV specials (about how onerous our tax burden was) to Americans being dragged off to prison for tax evasion, taxes grew and grew into an important part of our lives during the 20th Century. It's been calculated that we all work for roughly five months each year until we pay off our government obligations. Then, and only then, do we start working for ourselves.

Finally, in the late 1970's, Americans said, resoundingly, "Enough!" First, Howard Jarvis led a taxpayer revolt in California, our most populous state. Then we elected Ronald Reagan, who actually wanted to lower our taxes. Best of all, Reagan spent the political capital earned by the failed attempt on his life to enact significant across-the-board tax cuts.

For most of the past twenty years, many candidates ran for office promising lower taxes and reduced government spending. But now, things have changed.

The change is palpable in our focus groups. Recent generations are far more comfortable paying taxes – and even embrace the **concept** of taxation.

"I feel like it's the obligation of every citizen to pay taxes."
—Hilda, 56, Housewife, Apple Valley, MN

"I am happy to pay my taxes every year."
—Jill, 39, Part-Time Worker, Frisco, TX

Taxpayer resistance to federal taxation has, in fact, ebbed. Lowering our tax burden is not the priority that it once was.

"I rank taxes as ninth most important on this list [of priorities for government]."
—Sheila, 40, Daycare, Ocala, FL

"Taxes just aren't a big deal to me right now."
—Rusty, 48, Business Owner, Louisville, KY

Now, Americans certainly **aren't** enamored of big tax increases – that would clearly be a stretch. But taxes simply aren't on the radar screen like they were twenty years ago. It's more that taxes are a non-issue, not a negative issue, at least for most Americans. So however dissatisfied Americans profess to be with our government, taxes are not at the root of the dissatisfaction, at least right now. And that's a distinct change from the last thirty years in the United States.

But the real issue moving forward is what consequence this period of laissez faire taxation will have on our country. Based upon our focus group work, we can foresee how this will impact our country in at least a couple of different places.

- **Taxes will increase in the near-term**. The timing is definitely right for gradual increases in taxes – at least until voters begin to resist in any substantive fashion. To a tax-and-spend politician, this is as close to nirvana as things get. Taxes are not a high priority right now, and that's precisely why politicians will increase taxes soon; after all, they do the same polling as everybody else.

- **The size of government will continue to grow significantly, or roughly in step with tax increases, in the near future**. Why? Because taxes are literally the life blood of government – and politicians always find a way to spend tax money, don't they?

- **Another tax revolt is coming.** It's difficult to guess how far off, but it seems likely within the next five years, especially with the economic downturn of 2008. Sure, voters are not terribly motivated to lower taxes **right now**. But it won't last. And the more squeezed Americans feel financially, the more likely they are to question their expenditure on taxes. It's as inevitable as death and…well, you get it.

You Know Who To Blame

Okay, time for another quiz. Hint: This is an **easy** quiz.

Question: Who do you blame for…

- High taxes.
- The newest form of epilepsy.
- The latest terrorist attack in the world.
- Inadequate hurricane relief.
- Russia's foray into Georgia.
- The "do-nothing" Congress.

Answer(s): Why, flip over all the cards. You know the answer to all of these, don't you? Say it loud and say it strong: The government!

One of the major influences on government and politics in this era is the utter contempt we show for government at all levels, but especially the federal government. And the reason our quiz was so easy is that Americans blame the government for almost everything that goes wrong in our country, including all the items in the quiz, plus this smattering of quotes we dug out of the files:

"I blame the government for food prices."
—Tilda, 28, Housewife, Temecula, CA

"I blame the government for 9-11."
—Eli, 46, Accountant, New Rochelle, NY

"The government is responsible for the environment, absolutely."
—Sidney, 23, Teaching Assistant, Miami, FL

"All the bad weather we've had. You can blame the government for that."
—Cal, 39, Unemployed, Indianapolis, IN

"The government is responsible for the bad school lunches, for sure."
—Syd, 36, Delivery, South Memphis, TN

And why are we blaming the government for everything that goes wrong in life? The answer's not that clear, other than, like Mt. Everest, because it's there. In short, our focus groups do **not** indicate **why** people are so unhappy with government. We've asked the question in groups before, but have never gotten a clear answer.

So why should we care about this trend? Why bother mentioning it here? For two reasons. First, this "blame the government" habit is ultimately responsible for the low popularity ratings of the government, in general, and specific government entities, in particular. We live in such negative times, with respect to government, that anyone and anything connected to government are ultimately held in disrepute. And that can't be healthy – ultimately, we'll undoubtedly reject and/or vote out very capable people, simply out of habit.

Second, I'd expect this trend to ultimately link up with the tax issue. We certainly won't support a tax increase for the government if we are so unhappy with it, blaming the government for everything that goes wrong in life. Ultimately, this dissatisfaction will point toward tax cuts. And, based on the level of dissatisfaction, rather deep cuts, at that.

Mirror, Mirror...

The last major issue which is influencing our view of government in the United States is our expectation of America's role in the world. Specifically, we are seriously conflicted about what we want America to be in this world.

> *"I'm not sure how the world sees us [Americans] anymore."*
> —Boyd, 41, Semi-Retired, Los Angeles, CA

> *"I'm really not sure what we want the rest of the world to think about us [Americans] anymore."*
> —Stacy, 40, Housewife, Farmington, NM

Since we left our pre-World War II isolationism, and became the de facto leaders of the free world, America's role in the world has been fairly constant, sparking little debate. Our roles have included policemen to the world, moral leader, role model, and promoters of democracy, among others. But that all changed that tragic day in September of 2001. And that's why we're conflicted.

It's not clear what role Americans want the country to assert or assume in the future. Our old role is still unoccupied. But so are some other roles:

- **"Tough guy on the block"** – with our battle tested military.

- **"World disciplinarian"** – keeping other nations in line.

- **"Change Agent"** – specifically, to promote and lead (by example) with respect to changes in international relations.

- **"One Of The Boys"** – to promote that the U.S. is "just another country" on the international stage – not any better than other nations.

I am not a foreign policy expert, as you might have guessed from the preceding list. Regardless, it's clear that Americans are not walking with that swagger on the international stage these days. Once we figure out our role – including one that might not have made my list – the swagger will likely return.

Conclusion

While outlining this chapter, I started to recall one set of groups that I conducted many years ago, in Towson, MD (suburban Baltimore), on government policy. Long after the groups had ended – and I was cleaning up the focus group room – an elderly gentleman shuffled back into the room. He'd been very charming and helpful during the group, and so we started chatting like old friends. After about ten minutes, he finally turned to go. After all, it was getting late.

But before he'd left the room, he blurted out one more question – a question I still remember to this day. "Say," he said cheerfully, "what do you suppose we'd all have said about the government ten or twenty years into the future?"

I can't remember what I answered then. I'm sure I mumbled something.

But I can sure tell you what I'd answer now...

Regardless of who we are, where we live, or how we live, government exerts a **major** influence on our lives. From terrorism's life-or-death grip, to the simple act of paying a sales tax with your purchase of a Starbuck's coffee, there's really no escaping the influence of government in our daily lives.

If you can, flip back to the quotes that opened this chapter. With respect to Oscar Wilde's insightful quote, let's hope that most of our lives are spent discussing a good government, not a bad one, and especially not a **Raw Deal**. We can probably all agree on that.

"Life is rather like a tin of sardines – we're all of us looking for the key."
—Alan Bennett

Chapter 8:

The Rise Of The Freakin'

Springer Generation

☆ ☆ ☆ ☆ ☆

"As we peer into society's future, we – you and I and our government – must avoid the impulse to live only for today, plundering for our own ease and convenience the precious resources of tomorrow."
–President Dwight Eisenhower's Farewell Speech (January of 1961)

"Man, wouldn't it be cool if we were all nude during this focus group? It would be great if we could have a group-sex 'thing' on top of the [focus group] table after the focus group, wouldn't it?"
–Juice, 29, Unemployed, Storrs, CT

Somewhere In The 1950's

"Okay kids, now that dinner is done, let's do something really fun, okay?"

The kids screamed in delight as they ran from the linoleum-lined kitchen to the paneled family room. "What are we going to do, Dad?" Tommy, a lad of no more than twelve, but the oldest of this pack, bellowed. "What are we going to do, Dad?" he asked once again insistently, as if disbelieving that fun was on the horizon.

"Okay, kids, sit down on the couch," he said to his brood of five. "Come on in mother," he added to his lovely wife, still working on dishes. "Come on, before the fun starts," he added.

As his wife bounded into the room, he opened the closet, and rolled a large square article, covered in burlap, out into the middle of the room. Gasps were muted as the kids were just plain confused. What **was** this contraption?

"Okay, kids," the dad announced, seemingly oblivious to his wife, standing next to the sofa. After tugging for a few moments at the string that covered the TV, he finally started to pull the burlap off.

As the dad grabbed it from each end of the TV, and tugged the burlap over the top and onto the floor, the kids finally reacted.

"Wow," became the operative word, whether shouted (by the oldest brother, Tommy), or whispered by the younger girls. "Dad, wow," they almost seemed to shout in unison.

"A television!" Tommy screamed out. "A television," he screamed again, even louder. "A television," the younger kids squealed.

"That's right, kids. From now on, we can watch our very own TV, every night, right here. It'll be like our very own theatre," the father claimed while plugging it in, and turning the large dial to operate his theatre.

The room was quiet while the unit warmed up, until bold sound began pouring through the unit's tiny speakers.

"The NBC Television Network," an announcer intoned, while the NBC logo turned into a bird with plumes.

"Here," the father said, while twisting the dial. "Let's find CBS right now. I think there's a great show the whole family will enjoy," he added, sounding like his own promotion department. "Here. Here it is, kids."

Just then, the show's theme music tore into overdrive, announcing the start of...

"Kids, you're going to love this. I think this is the 'I Love Lucy' show. She's this crazy red-headed lady who gets into all kinds of trouble."

"So she's a really funny lady, daddy?" the man's youngest daughter asked while giggling, as if she could actually see the show **before** the show.

"Oh, you know it, sweetie," the man said as he gave his daughter a hug and a kiss. *"She is **really** funny."*

As the show started, the kids stared intently at the screen.

"Look, Daddy, those are women," one of the boys said.

"Yeah, and they're kissing each other!," another one shouted.

"Look it. There's a guy punching another guy in the head," one of the girls said. *"Is that Lucy? Or is she that other woman who's taking her shirt off?"*

All of a sudden, the family room was dead silent as they watched.

A girl named Amanda announced on the tube, *"You are the biggest bitch in the world."*

And with that, now it was the girls who started punching, as their bemused mail escorts watched from the side of the stage.

Then, an announcer intoned, *"Tomorrow on Springer, Lesbian Call-Girls Who Want To Have Sex-Change Operations."*

"Okay kids. Time for bed," the mother shakily announced as her face turned beet red. Suddenly, family TV night had ended.

The Springer Generation

Okay, readers, this is the part where they play the music that sounds like a violin tuning, and the screen turns blurry – you know, where you suddenly realize something really strange is happening – like, say, current talk show king Jerry Springer replacing 1950's TV icon Lucille Ball in a vicious time warp. And why is this happening, you wonder?

Because there is no better way to introduce… drumroll please… the [Jerry] **Springer Generation!.** During the course of our many focus groups over the past twenty years, we've noted the slow, steady rise of what we've now come to know as the Springer Generation, named in honor of talk-show host and former Cincinnati Mayor Jerry Springer. (A confession: I sometimes watch Springer and even find it entertaining at times.)

"My goal in life is to be on the Jerry Springer Show someday."
–Pasquale, 23, Unemployed, Des Plaines, IL

The reason that we've named this generation after Springer is simply because his TV talk show seems to embody the key qualities and characteristics of this emerging generation of Americans (although many don't watch the show regularly). Specifically, the Springerites, or Springer Generation, tend to be crude, rude and vulgar.

TRAITS OF THE SPRINGER GENERATION

1. Rude	5. Uneducated
2. Crude	6. Tacky/Uncouth
3. Vulgar	7. Foul-Mouthed
4. Tasteless	8. Violent

This is not meant to be an attack on Jerry Springer himself, his guests, or his audience. Far from it. One might even argue that Jerry Springer is a truly brilliant entertainer, who's figured out over the years how to moderate a talk show that appeals to our base instincts. From his guests' profanity-laced tirades, the stripper pole on the main stage, topless/nude guests and audience members, the distribution of Springer beads to topless female audience members, the fights, and even a mock reverend performing "weddings," Jerry Springer has certainly figured out how to produce an occasionally entertaining hour of television.

The problem isn't the Springer show itself. No, it is what it is. It's probably closer to satire than anything else. And as with any TV show, I always reason that if you don't like it, don't watch [TV] or turn the channel. And that certainly applies to Springer.

No, the problem is that the U.S. seems to have spawned an entire generation of Americans who **embody the Springer qualities and values, all the time** – not just when they watch the talk show. The Springer Generation essentially lives life like its one, long episode of the *Springer* show. And their influence on our society has become palpable over time.

Their influence on our focus groups has been undeniable – from foul-mouthed dialogue to sexual innuendos that sometimes distract from discussions. (Re-read the quote from our focus groups at the opening of the chapter.)

> *"I'm not sure I bleepin' agree with you, you bleep."*
> –Harry, 26, Unemployed, Boulder, CO

> *"How many ladies in here [in the focus group room] would like to have sex with me? C'mon ladies, don't be shy."*
> –Marquis, 38, Entrepreneur, Chicago, IL

The Springer Generation isn't necessarily a specific demographic group. While they probably tend to be a little younger, on average – for those are the people who tend to watch his highly-rated talk show – you can find Springerites from all age groups, ethnic groups and genders. For being a Springerite is essentially a state of mind. (A depraved state?)

Now, easy dear readers. I am not at all suggesting that the whole country is now Springerland. No, much like any other generation or movement, the Springer Generation is just a part of our country, not the whole country. In fact, many of us don't embody the qualities of the Springerites in any way, shape or form.

But the Springerites **do** exert a major influence on our country these days. Join me, dear readers, as we take a look around at our "Springerized" country: – that is, the coarse, often crude society that we've become:

- A study in the Journal of Adolescent Research showed that young adults are far more accepting of pornography than their parents, including college-age women embracing and accepting porn in record numbers.[23]

- U.S. Comptroller General David Walker was quoted in The Financial Times as saying that there are alarming parallels between the end of the Roman empire and the` United States of 2008. Walker claimed that there are "striking similarities" between the declining Roman empire and the U.S., including America's current declining moral values.[24]

- A Tarant County (Fort Worth, TX) grand jury indicted the owner of a popular **children's** amusement ride on multiple

---

[23] As reported by Kathleen Fackelmann, in USA Today, December 13, 2007.
[24] As reported in MSN Money Online, August 20, 2007.

counts of molesting the riders (children) – 12 indictments in all.[25]

- Staying in that area of the country, a 6 year-old Garland, TX girl won a national contest to see Disney star Hannah Montana in concert in New York, during one of 2007's most popular concert tours. The winning entrant wrote an essay about losing her father during combat in Iraq. The only problem was that the contest entrant did not lose her father in combat, didn't really have a father, and didn't even write the essay. Her Mom did. The girl's mother, reflecting the true spirit of the contest, claimed she did nothing wrong. "We wrote whatever we could do to win. [The contest rules] never said the story had to be true. We wrote whatever we could to win."[26]

- A radio promotion for a drive-time radio show in Denver, CO, in early 2008, referenced "camel toes." This is a rather graphic reference to a female body part. Nuff said.

- The American Society for Aesthetic Plastic Surgery reported that the number of women under the age of 18 who had undergone breast enlargement has soared over the past decade.

- BP, the world's third largest petroleum company, announced that its Chief Executive, John Browne, resigned after lying to

[25] Hundley,Wendy, *"Children's Ride Owner Indicted,"* Fort-Worth Star Telegram, December 30, 2007.
[26] Langton, Elizabeth, *"False Essay Wins Trip To See Pop Star,"* Fort-Worth Star Telegram, December 30, 2007.

a British judge about his homosexual relationship with another man.[27] (The problem isn't homosexuality – it's the lying in high court.)

- And the concept of school spirit certainly has changed for the Springer Generation. Teen pregnancy rates at Massachusetts' Gloucester High soared in 2008 amid reports that as many as several dozen girls at the school participated in a "pregnancy pact," a contest in which getting pregnant and giving birth was the goal.

- Who can forget that good old Springer violence? Well, certainly not the youth of America. In 2002, the last year for which we have complete stats, more than 8750,000 young people, ages 10 to 24, were injured in the U.S. from violent acts. Approximately 1 in 13 of these youngsters required hospitalization for the violent acts. Of course, homicide is the second leading cause of death with this age group (but the leading cause of death for African-Americans this age).[28]

Why, if we combine all of these points together, we'd have almost a complete week of Jerry Springer episodes!

But let's catch our breath for a moment – what does the rise of the Jerry Springer Generation really mean for our country? No need for a long list or a table to explain this one. The Springerization of America simply means that we now live in a country that is rude, crude and coarse – replete with foul language, rudeness, tackiness, violence, inappropriate

---

[27] Stinson, Jeffrey, *"BP Chief Resigns As Personal Life Goes Public,"* USA Today, May 2, 2007.
[28] Reported by U.S. Census Bureau.

sexual innuendo, and drug use, to name but a few aberrant behaviors, at every turn. In other words, America in 2008 is certainly different than the America of 1950 or 1980.

Not quite persuaded yet? Well, take a drive to the local shopping mall, and watch the drivers around you – see how many times someone makes an obscene gesture at you. (Hint: When they flip their middle finger at you, they are **not** signaling that you're number one!) Take a young child to a football or baseball game, and see how many times you cringe as the crowd around you casually drops f-bombs and other coarse language on your little one. Join your mom or your teenage daughter for a night of TV, and see how many times you blush. Go to the movies, and see how many people talk out loud during the flick, much less whether what they're talking about is safe for public consumption.

And that's what it's like to live among the Springerites – they continually infringe upon our rights to live the way we want with their in-your-face behavior. And America has moved from a cultured, civil society to a coarse, bawdy world.

When I was a young undergrad at the University of Denver, one of my sociology professors insisted that TV is a direct reflection of our values – who we are, how we live, and what we believe in ultimately ends up on the tube. While writing this chapter, I thought about my old Prof for a bit. And then I started thinking about TV. (It may surprise some of you to learn that you actually **can** think about TV!)

In my childhood, I remember shows like *The Brady Bunch, Here's Lucy, Nanny & The Professor* and *Gilligan's Island*. They were sitcoms, but very few episodes, if any, revolved around sex or making adults looks stupid. No, this was a gentler time, the era of the family sitcom. True, not all of the families portrayed on these shows were realistic, or looked like my family. But TV tended to portray an idealized version of our best selves – i.e., what we wanted to be in life. Watch TV Land or Nick at Nite, cable channels built around these shows – it was truly a golden era.

Conversely, think about TV today. First off, there isn't any time for healthy, wholesome family sitcoms on most networks, the majority of programming is vile reality fare, in which producers push contestants into artificial battles with other contestants. Ever see MTV's *The Real World?* It probably represents the high (or low?) of this genre.

Beyond reality shows, there are dramas about high school kids outsmarting their dimwitted, yet rich parents (*Gossip Girl, Privileged, Beverly Hills 90210*). And there are a whole bunch of shows about dead bodies – all of the *CSI* series, *NCIS, Bones,* and *Without A Trace.* If you're an actor who can play a good dead body, steady work can be had in Hollywood these days.

And daytime TV? Well, back in the day, it was sitcom re-runs and game shows. Today? Talk shows in which the host is running paternity tests on guests, the aforementioned *Springer,* and a whole bunch of legal shows, in which the participants are most definitely mad at each other. Almost makes you want to swear never to have a kid stay home from school sick, watching TV, doesn't it?

But perhaps the "poster child" TV show for the Springer Generation is MTV's Tila Tequila starring in *A Shot At Love.* Sounds romantic, doesn't it? Well, judge for yourself.

A Shot At Love is a reality dating show in which both men and women compete for a chance to win the heart of the bisexual hostess, Tila Tequila, a former nude magazine model. Along the way, there are always plenty of scantily clad people, some crude language and sexual innuendo. One can only imagine Lucille Ball spinning in her grave at this show.

Where Art Thou Springer?

The natural questions to ask at this point are: Who are these Springers? Where have they come from? And how does one become a Springerite?

Our work with the Springer Generation over the years indicates that Springerites come from all age groups, income levels and racial groups. In other words, we are all Springerites, at times. As we've already noted, the Springer Generation is far more a state of mind than a group that has any formal membership requirements. The only true membership requirement is that you act as crude and as rude as possible, at all times.

Anthropologically speaking, it's not exactly clear **why** the Springer Generation has emerged at this point in our country's history. But after years of study in our focus groups, we have been able to identify some factors which appear to account for the rise of the Springer Generation.

Reasons For The Rise Of The Springer Generation
The Rise Of '60's Radicals
Just Kick Back, Man
TV Is Our Guide
Outrageous Behavior Is Idolized

The Rise Of '60's Radicals – If there is a single word to describe 1960's radicals as parents, it's "permissive." The generation that once tuned in and turned on with their drugs, apparently has "tuned out" when it comes to parenting.

> *"I sure haven't parented the same way that I was brought up."*
> –Rocket, 60, Fitness Instructor, San Diego, CA

> *"I let my kids do whatever they want. It's the only way they'll grow up."*
> –Sharon, 58, Housewife, New York, NY

> *"I admit that I am very permissive with my kids."*
> –Herbie, 60, Government Employee, Sterling Hts., MI

> *"I pretty much just let my kids do whatever they want. I've never been good at saying 'no' to them."*
> –Eve, 62, Retired Dance Instructor, Highland Park, IL

We've done focus group after focus group through the years in which a parent claims in the introduction that they were/are a "hippy" or "flower child." At some point during the group, they will inevitably cop to major problems in parenting – from children in jail to children who are major drug users. It's always clear to us that '60's radicals are still unconventional in some form – and parenting is often the way they express their unconventional side. Accordingly, it seems that a generation or two of children have been left to adopt the manners and grace – or lack thereof – of the Springer generation. More's the pity.

Just Kick Back, Man – It's also true that acting like a Springerite is, for many people, simply the easiest thing to do. In other words, we often give in to our base instincts, instead of trying to be noble or principled. Like the fine gentleman quoted below:

> *"I pissed in the bushes on the way in [to the focus group facility]. I didn't know if you people would have a can in here, or nothing. I guess it will help the flowers to grow (said while laughing)."*
> –Rex, 50, Parole Officer, Houston, TX

To these people, the answer to the question, "Why act like a Springerite?" is easy enough. As Rex, the parole officer who'd watered the shrubbery outside the facility later said in that group in Houston, "Why not?" Indeed.

TV Is Our Guide – Many kids today – and we mean, say, under the age of forty or so – act like a guest on *Springer* simply because they don't know any better. (This is the childlike behavior which earns them the moniker, "kids.")

In focus groups, we've found that many respondents tell us that they've been, or are, heavy TV watchers. Perhaps they were latch-key kids, or home alone for long stretches. Regardless, they have – and many still do – watch five to ten hours of TV per day.

> *"Man, I don't know what I'd do without the tube. It sure keeps me company."*
> –Drew, 30, Technician, Bethesda, Maryland

> *"I have TV on all the time. I really can't live without it."*
> –Rachel, 36, Model, Flushing, NY

So who have their babysitters been? Who's taught them manners and such? Well, there's *Seinfeld's* Kramer, Jim Belushi, Kevin James, Ray Romano, MTV's *Real World,* Maury Povich, and any number of other TV stars and hosts. Don't confuse this group with people who teach manners and etiquette to the King of England. Nope – far from it.

When I was a kid, most mothers stayed at home tending to the kids. Now, you can draw your own conclusions as to the skill and effectiveness watching over kids. I can still remember to this day the laundry list of shows that we were forbidden from watching when I was a child:

- **Batman** – for its obvious violence.

- **The Three Stooges** – for their not-so-obvious violence. (Yes, Mom thought all those slaps and nose-twists might be something we'd copy in adulthood. Not that I haven't been tempted at times...)

- **The Newlywed Game** – I think I knew more about "Making Whoopee" than about sex until I finally went off to college.

- **Let's Make A Deal** – for its focus on greed and money.

Okay, okay, let's cut the list there, if for no other reason than to save **me** embarrassment. I can assure you that her actual list was a lot longer than this, in reality. And we weren't particularly religious, or particularly anything. She just thought she was being a Mom. And all my friends pretty much grew up the same way.

Fast forward to today, a time when many focus group respondents freely admit that they do not supervise or limit TV viewing in any way. Why, you ask? Well:

"There's no way that TV is as bad as what they'll experience in real life. So I just let 'em watch."
–Jamaal, 36, Counselor, Council Bluffs, IA

And Jamaal is far from alone. We find in interviews that parents supervise young kids, but after a certain age – say, ten – kids are given a free run with the TV

So next time any of you Americans start worrying about the future and our kids, relax. It's mostly TV that is babysitting – and teaching – our kids.

Outrageous Behavior Is Idolized – The last reason that Springerites have grown in prominence is because we tend to praise, reward, and even idolize people who are rude, crude, violent or nude. The more outlandish their behavior, the more we celebrate the perpetrator of such behavior.

There's a reason why Paris Hilton and Kim Kardashian have become mega-celebrities, largely for the release of unauthorized sex tapes. There's also a reason that death row inmates often get the whole hour on CNN's *Larry King Live*. And there's a reason that the media pursued the hooker who ruined Eliot Spitzer's once luminous political career. Ostensibly, she did little more than lie on her back in order to ruin the New York Governor's once-bright career. But tabloid TV still considered that an accomplishment.

So be careful next time you complain at City Hall or the FCC about an outlandish hour of *Springer*. Given our penchant for rewarding bad behavior, the Mayor or FCC Commissioner will likely be a former *Springer* guest.

The Future

As we've asked throughout the book, so where does our country go from here?

When I think of such questions, I always recall the scene in *Top Gun* in which Tom Cruise, after melodramatically going AWOL, asks base commander Tom Skerritt about his options.

"Simple" Skerritt replies immediately.

Well, the same is true here. When we ponder where the country should go after this bout of Springerism, the options are, to paraphrase Skerritt, simple.

On the one hand, we can do nothing, and allow our country to drift further into the Land of Springer. Will this mean stripper poles on Main Street? People in court duking it out to find a winner? Who knows? But the Springer Generation will get nothing but stronger and more influential, in this scenario.

On the other hand, if we, as a country, decide that enough is enough and want to change the quality of life in the USA, we can. It will be neither dramatic nor gut-wrenching. It simply requires that we not give in to basic instincts, and that we start behaving as if life is more than a lap dance or fight.

Where will we head in the future? Well, as they might say on Eyewitness News, "Stay tuned."

Farewell, Jerry Springer

When preparing to write this chapter, I checked the files to see how often Jerry Springer has been mentioned in our focus groups. Would it surprise you to learn that Springer has come up in hundreds of focus groups over the past five years? Perhaps, it wouldn't, if you studied the Nielsen ratings and saw that *Springer* is one of the highest rated daytime programs in American television, and that the talk-show host enjoys a fiercely loyal, devoted audience.

So while I've never moderated a focus group specifically devoted to Jerry Springer (Jerry, if you ever need help, call me!), you can see that he's often on the minds of the American public, in one way, shape or form.

I will never forget a focus group several years ago that was held at The Merchandise Mart in downtown Chicago, just a stone's throw away from where Jerry Springer actually tapes his show.

Somehow, the topic of **The Jerry Springer Show** had come up early in the group, and I'd let the group wail away at it, in an effort to build rapport, something that would come in very handy later in the group. But one particular respondent, Pepe, a delivery truck driver, built rapport all by himself. I can still remember his words to this day.

Listen, I really love the Springer show," Pepe told the room full of fellow focus group respondents. Then, becoming more impassioned, he noted, "I mean, I really love that show." The focus group respondents nodded in agreement.

Then, Pepe threw the room a curve, so to speak – especially me. "But just because I like Springer's show doesn't... ." Suddenly, Pepe simply stopped.

The focus group room was now dead silent.

"Just because I like Springer," he started again. And then suddenly, he stopped again, as if overcome with emotion. A few moments later, Pepe snorted and shook his head, but remained quiet.

Then, in a quiet voice, he started one more time. "Just cause I like the Springer show for entertainment doesn't mean that I want my friends to act that way, you know, like the guests on the show. And it doesn't mean I want any of that Jerry Springer stuff in my daily life. Know what I mean?"

The focus group respondents signaled or verbalized their agreement, vociferously, as if on a religious retreat. "You go, Pepe," one girl said with fervor.

"I mean, Jerry Springer is great," he allowed. "But," Pepe continued, "that doesn't mean I want him as part of my daily life. No way, man. I don't want my life to be anything like the Springer show." The focus group room roared their approval in response.

As I think today of profanity in public places, stripper poles, teen pregnancy, rudeness, crudeness, today's TV, violence and fistfights and the like, I can now tell you that I still roar my approval for Pepe's speech, as well. Great job! But it makes me wonder, what took us so long to say it?

Epilogue

☆ ☆ ☆ ☆ ☆

"This is the first age that has paid much attention to the future, which is rather ironic, since we may not have one."
—Arthur C. Clarke

"The future is looking pretty bleak, man. Pretty bleak."
—Fred, 41, Semi-Pro Football Coach, Missoula, MT

It took approximately one year to write this book. Often during this period, I stopped in at a local International House Of Pancakes for breakfast or dinner. Now, some of you may think of IHOP as just another chain restaurant. However, while writing the book, I began to think of it more as my neighborhood diner, a place where I soon knew the staff and could talk about the book during its formative stages.

I didn't necessarily go to IHOP regularly. Everyone writes differently, but I tend to strike while the iron is hot, and to read the paper and dine out when I don't feel in the mood (to write). In other words, I'm not one of those eight-hour-a-day, five-days-a-week writers. But I did go to IHOP more or less weekly. That's kind of regular.

It was during my many visits to IHOP that year that I befriended Joe, an 18-old veteran waiter at IHOP. Over the course of my visits, I learned that Joe had graduated from high school, and was heading to the University of Colorado in the fall. He was a very bright young kid, who took an interest in what I did for a living. Ultimately, I felt comfortable enough around Joe to mention this book.

To say that he was supportive and enthusiastic about the book was an understatement. Joe couldn't get over the fact that he knew an

actual author. (Some days, I can't, either.) As I look back, it seems that one of the reasons I headed to IHOP so regularly was the positive reinforcement I felt from Joe. After all, writing a book is one of the loneliest jobs in the world, as anyone who's tried, or actually written a book, will tell you.

One day, as I was standing at the counter and paying for another splendid club sandwich dinner, Joe and I started talking about the book again. Within moments, he was asking a question that I'd never heard before, or even thought about. Sure he knew what *America In Focus* was all about, but…maybe he knew it **too** well.

"So is your book real negative?" he asked innocently.

With that one question, I suddenly imagined that all activity in the tiny restaurant had ground to a halt. . maybe traffic on the busy street outside the restaurant had stopped, too. Maybe the whole world, for that matter.

"You know, cause if it's real negative, if it's a real downer, no one will want to read it," he continued while loading a tray of coffee cups onto the counter.

"So is it?" he persisted. "You know, negative?"

To this day, I have no idea what I answered, how I got home, or even how I got to bed. In fact, for a few days, I was in a complete trance. Suffice it to say, I didn't get any writing done, either. Joe had really thrown me for a loop – was the book entirely too negative? Maybe America really wasn't going to be in focus, after all.

But somehow, over the next few days, my thoughts crystallized. Finally, a few days after the fog had commenced, it blew right out of town and with it, and the paralysis in my life blew away, too. Suddenly, I had the answer to the negative issue.

I'm not sure if this book is positive or negative, overall. Ultimately, it doesn't really matter.

In retrospect, portions of this book probably are pretty negative – or at the very least, they aren't very uplifting. But as long as they are an accurate portrayal of what we've seen and heard in focus groups over the past twenty years, what's the harm? After all, as promised in the introduction, *America In Focus* is simply a reflection of who and what we Americans really are – both good and bad. In other words, this book was never intended as a fanciful, unrealistic portrayal of Americans; actually, it was designed to be quite the opposite.

Now, we get to the really good part. What if this is a rather unflattering picture of our country as we near the end of the first decade of the 21st century? In fact, what if this is a downright awful time to be an American? What if some of us really don't like the picture of America that emerges in *America In Focus*?

Well, as one my very first college political science professors at Loyola University once said, "Don't like it? Then change it, people."

And it's really not any more complex than that simple thought, for Joe the IHOP waiter, or anybody else, is it? If there are portions of our American lifestyle which we don't like, then it's up to us to change things. And the onus isn't on everybody else, my friends. It on **us,** as individuals. Change rarely starts at the top. Why, it's even difficult to achieve a majority consensus, much less to change. No, change starts at the bottom.

From politics to economics, and even social issues, if we don't like the way things are, we need to change things, starting with ourselves. And that's the beauty and simplicity of how each of us can respond to *America In Focus*. It's a bit like checking your wardrobe in the mirror. *America In Focus* is nothing if not a giant reflection, or mirror, of who we Americans are, based on talking to literally tens of thousands of Americans, from every area of the country, over the course of roughly twenty years. What we like, we can maintain. But whatever we don't find flattering in our fun-house size reflection, we can most definitely work to change.

In the end, reading *America In Focus* should help strengthen us, not weaken us, by helping to make things better. What we like, we'll keep. And that part of the American experience which we don't like, we can change. And I will forever be grateful to Joe at IHOP for having helped me to reason through this, and for even bringing the "negative" issue to the surface. I can only imagine how bright Joe's future will be, in college and beyond.

Contemporary American mogul Ted Tuner – yes, **that** Ted Turner – once observed, "Life is like a B-movie. You don't want to leave in the middle of it, but you don't want to see it again." Oh, how wrong Turner was. Whether simply looking at our giant reflection in the mirror occasionally, using this book to see what we can change about America, or even going to another twenty years of focus groups, hundreds per year, to build on our work in this book, I can't wait to see *America In Focus*, again and again, and even again. Join me?

About The Author

✮ ✮ ✮ ✮ ✮

Robert J. Burgess is the Founder and President of Marketing Advocates, Inc., one of the country's largest, most respected and innovative focus group/market research firms. Since 1990, Marketing Advocates, Inc. has worked with some of the biggest and best known companies worldwide, conducting both surveys and focus groups on a wide variety of subjects.

Mr. Burgess previously authored, *Silver Bullets: A Soldier's Story Of How Coors Bombed In The Beer Wars*, an acclaimed look at beer marketing. Published in 1993, the book has generated worldwide interest in the beer industry.

When not traversing the globe in search of a great marketing concept or the answer to a vexing problem, Mr. Burgess is a hopeless romantic and rabid sports fan, a combination that never fails to get him in trouble.

Mr. Burgess is currently single, and resides in suburban Denver, his home since 1980. Find out more about him at:

www.marketingadvocates.com

The Focus Group Guy™ goes to work on another group.

www.ingramcontent.com/pod-product-compliance
Lightning Source LLC
Chambersburg PA
CBHW020609270326
41927CB00005B/240